European Capital Markets

European Capital Markets

Werner G. Seifert
Ann-Kristin Achleitner
Frank Mattern
Clara C. Streit
Hans-Joachim Voth

EUROPEAN CAPITAL MARKETS

St. Martin's Press, Scholarly and Reference Division, 175 Fifth Avenue, New York, N.Y. 10010

First published in the United States of America in 2000

Printed in Great Britain

ISBN: 0–312–23382–5

Library of Congress Cataloging-in-Publication Data
European capital markets / Werner G. Seifert ... [et al.].
p. cm.
Includes bibliographical references and index.
ISBN 0–312–23382–5 (cloth)
1. Capital market—Europe. 2. Financial institutions—Europe. I. Seifert, Werner G.
HG5422 .E978 2000
332'.0414'094—dc21

00–021521

Contents

List of Figures and Tables

TABLES

List of Abbreviations

ABS	asset-backed securities
AEX	Amsterdam Stock Exchange
AMEX	American Stock Exchange
BAKred	Bundesaufsichtsamt für das Kreditwesen
BBA	British Bankers' Association
BIS	Bank for International Settlement
BoE	Bank of England
bp	basis point(s) (1/100 of 1 per cent)
CAGR	cumulative average growth rate
CBOT	Chicago Board of Trade
CEO	Chief Executive Officer
CFTC	Commodities Futures Trading Commission
CSFB	Credit Suisse First Boston
DBAG	Deutsche Börse AG
DTB	Deutsche Terminbörse (now Eurex)
ECB	European Central Bank
EFRP	European Federation for Retirement Provision
EMU	European monetary union
Euribor	European Interbank Offered Rate
Euro MTS	Italian government bond trading system
FED	foreign earnings deduction
FIBV	International Federation of Stock Exchanges
FRAs	floating rate notes
FSA	Financial Services Authority
IFC	International Finance Corporation
IFR	Institute for Fiscal Research
IMF	International Monetary Fund
IPO	initial public offering
ISD	Investment Services Directive
ISDA	International Securities Dealers Association
KonTraG	*Gesetz zur Kontrolle und Transparenz im Unternehmensbereich*
LBO	Leveraged buyout
Libor	London Interbank Offer Rate
LIFFE	London International Financial Futures Exchange
M&A	mergers and acquisitions
MBHC	multibank holding company
MBS	mortgage-backed securities

MGI	McKinsey Global Institute
MSCI	Morgan Stanley Capital Index
NYSE	New York Stock Exchange
OAT	obligation assimilable du trésor
OECD	Organization for Economic Co-operation and Development
ONS	Office of National Statistics
OTC	over-the-counter
p/e	price-earnings multiple
ppp	purchasing power parity
R&D	research and development
RTGS	real-time gross settlement
S&P	Standard and Poor's
SDC	Securities Data Company
SEC	Securities Exchange Commission
Soffex	Swiss Options and Financial Futures Exchange (now Eurex)
SPO	Seasoned Equity Offering
TFP	total factor productivity
Y2K	Year 2000

Preface

Interest in capital markets has increased almost as rapidly in recent years as share prices have. The quality and range of available statistics and the scope of public discussions about financial services, however, have not quite kept up with the bull run. Four of us first found ourselves confronted with the statistical 'fog of battle' and the difficulty of finding comparable figures for many key questions when we wrote a book about share ownership and the potential advantages of bringing a more vigorous equity culture to Germany. The problem is particularly acute in the case of studies comparing the competition of Europe's financial centres. In addition to the difficulty of finding or constructing comparable series, the problem is compounded by a lack of consensus on what factors should be examined to determine how successful individual financial centres are.

This book attempts to tackle some of the problems. We have used a wide range of statistics that facilitate more than a simple assessment of competitive positions. The results are by no means perfect – a team of authors cannot replace the work of statistical bureaux, which at the moment seem more concerned with collecting data on the physical outputs of Europe's 'sunset industries' than information about the service sector. In addition, we try to present some estimates of the benefits that countries derive from playing host to internationally important financial centres. Having examined the competitive positions of London, Frankfurt and Paris today, we discuss in some more detail the main factors driving change in the race for the premier financial centre in the European time zone. In the spirit of MIT economist Paul Krugman, we hope that, with some luck, our conclusions will annoy a few people. Many people hold strong views about which financial centre is ahead, and what will or will not allow relative positions to change – and careful reflection on the most relevant performance indicators or the main determinants of success is a little less common. It is in the hope of encouraging debate on these issues that this book has been written.

We owe a great debt to the many people who helped us write this book. Andreas Bergius in Barcelona, Giovanni Facchini in Stanford, Sara Horrell in Cambridge, Penny Butler in London, Aglaia Wieland at the European Business School in Oestrich-Winkel, and Norbert Funke, Ralf Schnellinger and Florian Neinert at McKinsey FIG Research in Frankfurt all contributed good ideas, crucial numbers and important suggestions. Ulrich Meißner and Terry Gilman commented on the typescript. We would also like to thank the many professionals who gave us so much of their valuable time – discussing ideas, providing information and reading sections of the typescript.

Frankfurt and Cambridge, November 1999

Executive Summary

The competition between European financial centres is a subject of spirited public debate. Has the introduction of the euro undermined London's position? Does tax competition disadvantage the continental centres? Should the regulation of institutional investment firms be changed? Is it good policy for governments to promote their national financial centres? And would the UK joining the European monetary union (EMU) threaten the position of continental centres?

This book seeks to provide answers to some of these questions that are currently confronting policymakers and industry players. We begin by assessing the competitive performance of Europe's three main financial centres – London, Frankfurt and Paris. According to our estimates, the City of London is approximately five times the size of either one of its continental rivals. In most areas, London appears ahead by a substantial margin – it often does more business than both of its competitors combined.

At the same time, continental centres have made great strides over the past decade. Many of the most harmful regulatory barriers have been removed; the size of financial communities, the quality of supervision, and the professionalism of players have improved markedly. Present trends, however, do not suggest that the City's demise as Europe's premier financial centre is likely any time soon. Talk of Frankfurt 'overtaking' London is the result of wishful thinking, not hard-headed analysis. We argue that competing head-on may not be sensible for financial centres such as Frankfurt and Paris. The stifling level of income taxation continues to hinder the flow of talent to the continent. Also, the momentum created by having a critical mass of talent, support services, and product volume will continue to act in the City's favour.

In many product areas, the UK's lead appears to be lengthening. These are not always the most attractive product areas – London is strongest where economies of scale and scope count the most, and it is in these product areas that margins are under severe pressure, and precious risk capital is required in large amounts. Continental competitors appear to be gaining ground in skill-intensive, high-margin businesses such as mergers and acquisitions (M&A) and equity issuance. Not only are these profitable and rapidly growing business areas; they are also of considerable benefit to continental economies, where restructuring is imperative and changes in capital structure are likely to release substantial value.

Much remains to be done before Europe can fully harness the power of capital markets. We make a number of suggestions. Even after the introduction of the euro, much remains to be done to create a unified European capital market. Regulatory change – possibly through the creation of a single financial services regulator – is urgently needed. We recommend a way in which the problem of high rates of income taxation on the continent could be circumvented. Also, the nascent restructuring of Europe's industries could be accelerated by a number of measures. Ultimately, quantum leaps ahead in terms of financial centre performance and the influence and quality of continental European capital markets are possible. Policymakers should make every effort to accelerate these developments. The benefits are likely to be substantial – but toppling London as the premier financial centre in the time zone will not be one of them.

1 Introduction

Financial centres are the physical location where capital markets are organized. Financial centres and capital markets are neither a cancer on the real economy nor are they simply providers of an alternative funding mechanism for local firms and governments. Financial systems serve to:

- pool savings and transform them into investment in plant and people
- discipline management, thus reducing the principal/agent problem
- allow the aggregation and trading of risk
- provide the information necessary for effective capital and risk allocation.

Capital markets are only one way of providing many of these functions, so they compete directly with banks and other financial intermediaries that provide them in-house.[1] There is, however, increasing evidence to suggest that capital markets are in some ways better at providing these essential functions. Financial centres makes a number of contributions. First, there are important externalities derived from their presence. Although this is potentially the most significant contribution they can make, it is also hardest to assess accurately. A number of studies strongly suggest that growth of output and productivity is significantly correlated with the extent to which the financial system is based on markets. The World Bank has concluded that, in a cross-section of 47 countries, productivity growth was faster in the economies with large, vibrant equity markets. Other authors demonstrate that a larger share of external financing provided by capital markets leads to faster growth of old firms, a more rapid growth in the number of young firms and accelerated structural change (see Box 1.1). In addition, a thriving financial centre can generate important export earnings, stabilizing the external value of a currency and covering deficits in other parts of the trade balance.

Second, financial centres create consumer surplus. For example, clients may be prepared to spend higher amounts on particular services than they actually have to. The difference between the 'reservation price' and the actual market price represents a windfall gain for these users of financial products. The price of some products varies considerably between countries; differences in competitive pressure are largely responsible. Idiosyncratic differences in fee levels are not only a distributional issue,

1

with financial intermediaries capturing a larger share of the pie. More importantly, high fee levels in countries with underdeveloped markets for some wholesale products also depress product demand, leading to net welfare losses.

Third, despite the fact that markets themselves have become increasingly virtual, the people employed by intermediaries, clients and service-providers still need to work somewhere, and they create value in their own right by performing services for the economy at large. Total value added is a first approximation of the contribution. The number of employees in wholesale financial services tends to be small; only in countries where the world's leading financial centres are located does the number of jobs created even approach that in other major industries. Of course, without job opportunities in financial services, most employees would not be unemployed; they would simply find a job elsewhere. But earnings per head in financial services are amongst the highest in any industry; this is particularly true after a run of good years, as in the recent past. Nor are high compensation packages the flip side of the coin of low profitability, since both profits (and tax paid) tend to be high. The differential between the value created in financial services, on the one hand, and the alternative creation of value if factors of production were put to other uses, on the other, is arguably the lowest possible value that can be put on the existence of thriving centre.[2]

The question that ultimately underlies these considerations for many of the smaller and medium-sized countries of continental Europe, at least, is the need to decide what is more important: to have a financial 'centre' of their own, or to have access to the services provided by a world-class centre.

Box 1.1
Finance and growth

The role of financial markets in fostering growth and development used to be either neglected or called into question. Joan Robinson famously remarked that 'where enterprise leads, finance follows', and other authors such as the Nobel laureate Bob Lucas argue that many economists 'badly over-stress' the role of financial factors in economic growth.[3] The same cannot be said any more. Recent research conducted under the auspices of the World Bank and at the University of Chicago indicates that there is a strong, causal link between the development of the financial sector, on the one hand, and economic development, on the other. There is new evidence at the macro- and the micro-economic level.

Recent studies by Levine et al. have used growth regressions based on the experience of 47 countries between 1976 and 1993.[4] They found a significant association between the state of financial development – measured either as the value of all shares traded relative to gross domestic product (GDP), or as bank credit relative to GDP – on the one hand, and economic growth, on the other. Both measures of financial system development are significantly correlated with growth, suggesting that they are not substitutes. Rather, they appear to serve different financing needs, thus facilitating growth. Interestingly, the equity market indicator appears to have relatively greater influence. For every 10 percentage-point increase in the value of shares traded, the growth rate of output in the cross-section of countries analysed by Levine goes up by a little less than 1 per cent. Interestingly, most of the increase is driven not by a higher rate of capital growth, as might have been supposed, but by faster productivity growth. Larger, more liquid equity markets therefore push the ultimate 'lever of riches' – productivity.[5]

There are a number of reasons why it is sensible to believe that the observed correlation points to a causal connection. First, the explanatory variable used is the level of stockmarket activity at the beginning of the period, and even if stock prices are a leading indicator for cyclical upturns to some extent, it appears unlikely that they act in this way with a horizon of 18 years. Second, if market capitalization is included in the regressions, the value of shares traded/GDP remains significant. Hence, the price level effect reflected in the market capitalization is not driving the result.

The evidence assembled by the World Bank receives further support from a study by Rajan and Zingales.[6] They ordered industry according to their 'capital hunger', that is, the extent to which they require outside finance for investment. High-growth industries constitute a large share of the group with the highest financing needs. In countries with large, vibrant stockmarkets (and transparent accounting systems), growth was systematically bigger for firms with large external financing needs. Not only did existing firms in states with highly developed capital markets grow their sales more rapidly than in countries with inadequate financial systems, but there were also more of them. Within a few years, firms in the same industry, but located in countries with different financial systems, differed markedly in terms of number and size.

DISINTERMEDIATION, CONSOLIDATION AND TECHNOLOGICAL CHANGE – FINANCIAL CENTRES IN THE 1990S

Three main forces have shaped the evolution of financial services in the 1990s. Disintermediation is increasingly undermining the traditional role of banks, aggregating savings and allocating capital. Firms are increasingly tapping the capital markets directly; institutional investors are becoming ever more powerful, and retail investors buy shares on-line or via low-cost index-tracker funds. Concentration within the industry has meant that a rapidly increasing share of most investment-banking business goes to a global 'bulge-bracket'.[7] At the same time, the rising importance of direct distribution capabilities has caused investment banks to link up with retail brokerages, or to join forces with commercial banks. The recent repeal of the Glass-Steagall Act suggests that this trend is likely to accelerate. The third force for change is the spread of electronic trading technology, making access to the world's most liquid markets from anywhere in the world a distinct possibility.

When Charles P. Kindleberger wrote his classic analysis of the formation of financial centres in 1974, he could point to a number of factors that made it compelling to concentrate all financial services in one physical location. The simple business of clearing cheques was best performed if all financial institutions have head offices in the same city – which is why, eventually, the Midland Bank, the Crédit Lyonnais and Dresdner Bank came to have head offices in cities other than the ones where they had been founded.[8] Financial services other than deposit-taking, lending and transferring money simply followed suit – driven towards the same degree of concentration by the synergies of the universal banks that had such a strong influence in many nineteenth-century economies.[9]

That financial service providers and users should operate in the same physical location is no longer a foregone conclusion. Although until recently physical proximity to markets was an important factor, the reasons for not locating in Milton Keynes, Freiburg or Nice have become less obvious. All the same, investment bankers and their clients accept the considerable expense of locating in financial centres, and high rents, long commutes, urban congestion and pollution all have to be weighed against the benefits. The main reasons why financial services continue to be concentrated in one physical location is that it reduces information costs, increases competition, and is a spur to innovation due to the benefits of specialization. In addition, achieving critical mass in one location can make it easier to attract talented personnel. Finally, locations become associated with certain product skills, or other advantages, allowing firms to effectively 'co-brand' their services by operating out of a respected financial centre. As is being recognized in other high-technology, high-skill industries, there are important advantages to such clustering.

The move towards financial centres appears to have accelerated in recent years. Many investment banks and securities firms are consolidating their operations in one physical location. Three factors are mainly responsible. First, the increasing use and sophistication of electronic trading systems, and of telecommunications more generally, make it possible to conduct many businesses from any location around the globe. There is no need to locate in the same place where orders for securities can be matched and executed; access to trading has become a part of the general infrastructure, not unlike the services of utilities. Second, Europe has seen considerable deregulation of financial services following the Investment Services Directive (ISD) in 1992, allowing firms with licences in one European member country to offer their services in another. Regulatory barriers therefore no longer make it necessary to establish a local office in the same jurisdiction as the client. Third, financial intermediaries are increasingly subject to severe cost strictures. Fees have fallen for many investment products, and the cost of good staff has increased considerably. Institutional investors often have considerable market power, and are increasingly likely to match the sophistication of investment banks. The need to trim costs in general has led many firms to rethink their physical presence in a large number of locations; infrastructure-providers such as exchanges and clearing houses have come under pressure to streamline their operations and offer one-stop services for a variety of European products. All three factors operate to encourage and facilitate the concentration of a firm's operations in one centre.

However, although a tendency towards centralization is evident, where the firms will choose to locate is less clear. Does concentration mean that banks will choose to put their operations in the domestic financial centre, or are other forces at work that make it more desirable to establish operations in some centres than others? The performance of individual 'capital cities' in relation to the changes in the associated product markets is examined in this book, and location decisions are related to their causes. Both the quality of market infrastructure and the momentum that comes from an existent concentration of services can have an immediate impact on these decisions. The fairness, quality and cost-efficiency of regulated markets continue to be at the very heart of the wholesale banking industry. However, the influence of this factor on decisions to locate in one place or another will diminish over time as remote access to cash and derivatives markets spreads. We examine the extent to which the importance of this factor is changing and look at how far size and momentum are driving changes in competitive positions.

There are, indirectly, a number of factors that impede or facilitate the growth of individual centres. Most prominently amongst them, regulatory barriers and tax issues can have a major impact on cost structures, the ability to conduct business and to innovate. Financial services, possibly more than any other industry, also depend crucially on the human capital of the workforce. Skilled, imaginative and ambitious people drive innovation and expansion. Ensuring a flow of such people into the centre is fundamental and this can be influenced by tax regimes, cultural issues and reputation. This book provides an appraisal of their impact on attracting people to places. But location is not just determined by supply-side elements – demand for the services of course also exerts an influence.

The structure of demand is significantly influenced by the strength of the domestic economy and regulatory conditions. Industrial structure, growth potential, export orientation, financing options and established corporate governance mechanisms will all have an impact on the demand for financial services by firms. Household demand too can vary across countries. Aspects such as pension provision, tax incentives and devolution of investment decisions to institutional managers are important. In one of the following sections, we also examine the financial literacy of the public at large, together with the returns achieved by investors, in order to gauge the level and quality of demand for financial services.

STRUCTURE

We first attempt to provide a firm empirical basis for examining the competitive position of individual financial centres as well as the evolution of capital markets. Of Europe's 'capital cities', we focus mainly on three: London, Paris and Frankfurt. Where comparisons are possible, Zurich is added to the analysis. Evidence from New York is used to provide a standard of comparison. We present statistics that allow us to assess the present position and future outlook for each centre, by using a combination of published statistics and surveys. The final result is not a single number summarizing all aspects of a centre's position, but a competitive profile in a number of dimensions. Chapter 2 looks at how individual financial centres perform in product areas such as over-the-counter (OTC) derivatives, M&A and bond trading. As part of the competitive profile, export performance and the ability of centres to attract financial service professionals are also considered.

Chapter 3 assesses the contribution made by financial centres and capital markets to the economies of their host countries. We look at both the direct benefits from financial centres in terms of the employment and value added, as well as the indirect benefits, which are primarily the efficient financing of industry, better capital allocation, more efficient trading of risks and the mobilization of investors' savings.

In Chapter 4 we analyse the competitive dynamics underlying the trends in the recent past, as well as possible changes in the future. The forces driving changes in different product areas are not uniform. They arise from factors such as technological developments, changed financing and investment opportunities, convergence of regulatory regimes and the adoption of the single currency. These aspects are analysed in some detail.

A better understanding of the nature and intensity of competition, and of the specific strengths and weaknesses of individual centres, can serve to guide policy and provide crucial information to the major players in the industry. Given the way the industry is developing, what is the best way forward? In Chapter 5, various feasible and relatively simple policy initiatives are described that could strengthen domestic financial centres, and facilitate growth and development by enhancing the efficiency of capital markets.

2 Performance Measures

This chapter first analyses the competitive performance of financial centres in the recent past in two categories: their ability to attract talented personnel and to capture market share in important product areas. We begin by discussing the most vital resource in investment banking and related businesses, highly skilled professionals. It is people who generate revenues and come up with the ideas, for instance to create new markets. How they are distributed by centre is one of our main topics.

Second, using the best available data, the market shares captured by individual financial centres in the most important product areas are assessed as if they were companies competing for customers. Strictly speaking, this is only true in the fully globalized product areas – such as forex and OTC derivatives trading, as well as bond trading and (partly) cross-border lending. In forex trading, for example, there is no particular reason to conduct business in one specific location. The same does not apply in other product areas, where some part of total value added has to be provided locally, such as the mergers and acquisitions (M&A) business. The position of individual centres is considered on a product-by-product basis, beginning with the most globalized markets. Figures for financial service exports are examined as a measure of financial centre performance in internationally contestable markets. For products with a significant local component, changes in domestic market size are discussed. This is not as accurate as estimates of actual market share captured by the centres in question, since it measures market size by country and not the proportion of services provided domestically; however, given the dearth of reliable data, it constitutes a good second-best.[10]

TOP TALENT

Although investment banking is a uniquely people-driven business, increasingly the advantages of a large capital base and good distribution matter as well, as evidenced by the recent wave of mergers in the US between investment banks and brokerage firms. Merrill Lynch benefits considerably from its retail network, and Goldman Sachs recently filled its 'war chest' with an initial public offering (IPO) for future acquisitions. Nonetheless, it is the skill and commitment of individuals that often makes the difference between success and failure, between trading profits and losses, and between clients returning or taking their business elsewhere. People are, in fact, what make financial centres successful – or not. In the age of virtual markets, it only matters to a limited extent where the computers stand that match orders and settle trades. By far the largest part of the value added in a particular financial centre is determined by the number and quality of individuals that it attracts.

Employment

Employment figures in financial centres are notorious only for their unreliability. Many a confident boast, such as the claim that there are more people employed in investment banking in London than there are inhabitants of Frankfurt, only belie the acute shortage of trustworthy numbers. Figures collected by national bureaux tend to focus on all employment in financial services, including retail banks (and often insurance as well as other business services).

The number of senior executives in investment banks can, however, be examined with some accuracy. Euromoney has compiled a directory of names, by functional area and location, of the top investment bankers in Europe. Although this is not a perfect measure of the allocation of personnel to towns, it does represents a telling indicator overall. The universe of sampled specialists is slightly wider than ideal, since staff in general management functions, as well as in retail banking, are included. There is

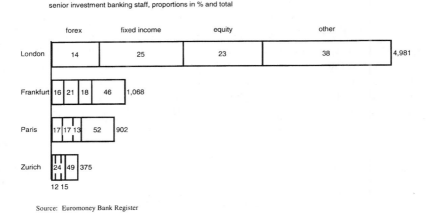

senior investment banking staff, proportions in % and total

Source: Euromoney Bank Register

Figure 2.1   Senior investment bankers by location, 1998

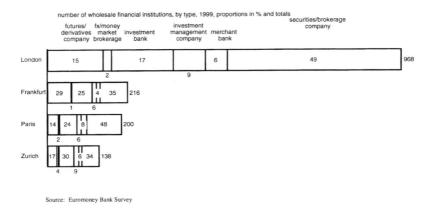

Source: Euromoney Bank Survey

Figure 2.2   Financial institutions by centre, 1998

a detailed breakdown by function and asset class, that is, fixed income derivatives, equity sales and forex trading. The staff listed are almost exclusively from the upper echelons of the business, such as fund management directors and heads of equity trading. These will be analysed below in their respective product areas. In this section, we simply deal with the totals and the scorecard overall.

Figure 2.1 gives an overview of the main results of the Euromoney survey. London is approximately five times larger than either one of its continental rivals, and records especial strengths in equity and fixed income. Frankfurt and Paris show some strength in fixed income, and report lower proportions in equity-related functions than London. Zurich follows at a respectable distance. How convincing is our analysis – that is, how likely is it that London as a financial centre is approximately five times the size of Frankfurt or Paris? Figure 2.2 records the number of financial institutions that are active in wholesale markets, by centre. The ordering of the centres is the same as in Figure 2.1, and the relative magnitudes are very similar: the senior staff numbers suggested a ratio of 100:21:18, and the respective number for the presence of relevant financial institutions is 100:22:21.

Access to Information

The number of banks is a crucial element for a successful financial centre, but what about the quality of the staff employed? There can be no direct measure of this, but looking at access to and use of the kind of information that tends to give people an edge – regular reports, the latest quotes, insightful analysis, expert interviews, and so on, is indicative. These are found in the specialized financial press, and from electronic information systems such as Bloomberg.[11] Figure 2.3 compares these four indirect indicators of the size of financial centres.

percentage of total in all three financial centres, in %

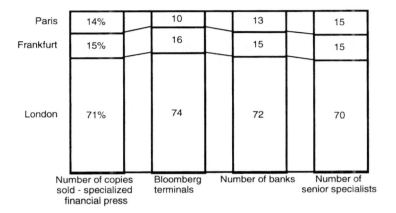

Figure 2.3   Bums, banks and brains, 1998

The relative size of individual centres is remarkably constant whether we focus on the number of specialist financial publications read, the number of Bloomberg screens used, or the staff and bank numbers.[12] In each and every category, London is larger than its two continental rivals put together, leading its nearest competitor, Frankfurt, by a factor of approximately 5:1. Just as consistent is the ranking for continental rivals – Frankfurt is ahead of Paris in all four categories, but the margin varies from 6 percentage points (Bloomberg screens) to less than 1 percentage point (number of senior specialists).

PRODUITS SANS PATRIE

For this first group of products that we analyse, location is of minimal importance. The goods are mostly homogenous, with prices easy to establish from any place on the globe. Trading these products makes few demands on market infrastructure.

Foreign-exchange Trading

In many ways the most 'globalized' product area of all is forex. The number of parameters influencing the price is minimal, liquidity is extremely high, and it can be traded in almost any location that does not impose stringent foreign-exchange controls. Much of the trading used to be performed over the telephone as multilateral price discovery (as is normally performed on exchanges) was unnecessary. In recent years, electronic systems such as Reuters 3000 and those provided by the Group of 30 leading banks have gained ground.

The value of forex trading has reached very high levels in recent years. On an average day in April 1998, the equivalent of more than one-quarter of US GDP changed hands between players in the market. Trading has almost tripled in magnitude since the late 1980s, with total world forex trading growing at an annual rate of 15.5 per cent.

Average daily turnover, US$ bn

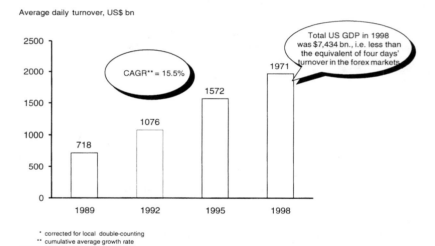

* corrected for local double-counting
** cumulative average growth rate
Source: BIS

Figure 2.4   Total net-gross* foreign-exchange turnover per year, selected years 1989–98

Dealing with currencies traded, first it should be noted that the latest Bank for International Settlement (BIS) figures are from 1998, so there is no new information yet on the role of the euro. In 1998 the largest share of the total currencies traded were transactions in US dollars. DM transactions came second, with 15 per cent of the total. Yen transactions and other currencies made up the remaining 41 per cent. The imbalance was smaller in the case of spot transactions, where the dollar led by 39 per cent to 21 per cent for the DM. The dollar's dominance was most pronounced in forex swaps, where nearly half of all transactions involved the dollar on one side. Given that forex swaps accounted for more than half of the total, the overall total was strongly influenced by this specific category. Most business conducted on the forex market involves cross-border transactions between dealers. Here Germany recorded the highest proportion of foreign dealers acting as counterparties (69.7 per cent), and the US the lowest (33.4 per cent). Non-financial customers were the counterparties in the smallest percentage of all transactions (with the exception of France and the US).

However, although dollars and DM were the predominant currencies traded and Germany had the largest proportion of cross-border interactions, this does not translate into similar importance for the places where the trading itself occurs. Most of forex trading is concentrated in three financial centres. Between them, the US, UK and Japan account for 58 per cent of total forex trading. Over time, this concentration ratio has not changed markedly. Concentration fell slightly between 1989 and 1992, from 57 per cent to 54 per cent. But since 1992 it has rebounded by 4 percentage points. The performance of individual countries has, nonetheless, diverged. The US and the UK pulled ahead of the pack by an increasing margin between 1992 and 1998, with most of the gains accounted for by UK performance.[13] The UK increased market share by around 5 percentage points, the US gained 2 percentage points and Japan lost 2 percentage points.[14] London took an impressive 32 per cent of global forex turnover, and was ahead of the second-best competitor by 14 per cent (up from a lead of 11 per cent in 1992). Switzerland and Hong Kong lost one-third of their market share in the same period, Germany largely managed to hold its own and France gained (Figure 2.5).

In 1998 the UK and the US led in all three major currencies. However, the UK's dominance was strongest in US dollar and DM transactions, where it accounted for 32–34 per cent of total transactions, and weakest in yen trades (where its market share was a mere 22 per cent). Germany showed a strong position in DM transactions, capturing 10 per cent of the market, but was a small player in US dollar and yen business. Of course, exposure to a devaluing yen would have an adverse impact on the market share of those countries that deal most in this currency. However, Germany's market share remained static, having had a small exposure to the yen, whilst London managed to grow despite a moderate exposure. Without the currency movements, London's lead over Germany would have

In % of total turnover, daily totals 1992 and 1998, US$ bn

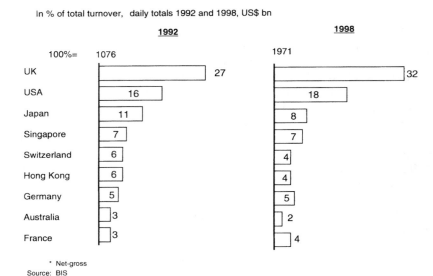

* Net-gross
Source: BIS

Figure 2.5   Shares in total forex trading,* 1992 and 1998

In % of European total, daily totals US$ bn

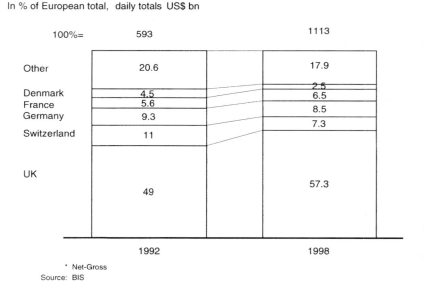

* Net-Gross
Source: BIS

Figure 2.6   Market share in total forex trade* in Europe, 1992 and 1998

Without the currency movements, London's lead over Germany would have been bigger.

In transactions with non-financial customers, the UK took second place, behind the US. Britain's market share was equivalent to 18.4 per cent. Germany and France also registered lower market shares in this type of transaction than in the overall market, and the US took a disproportionately high share.

Slightly more of the world forex trade was conducted in Europe in 1998 than in 1992, with Europe's share rising from 55 per cent to 56.5 per cent. This implies that most of London's gains in forex trade came at the expense of its European rivals. In 1998 the UK accounted for more than half of total European currency trading. With the exception of France, all other European countries lost ground compared with 1992. Not one of London's competitors managed to capture more than 10 per cent of European forex trading.

The composition of staff by functional area is shown in Figure 2.7. Forex research is much more concentrated than forex trading, with five out of six European specialists sitting in London. In trading, London had 5.5 times Frankfurt's staff, and approximately 4 times that of Paris. This tallies well with the trading figures, where London recorded 6.4 times Frankfurt volumes. Aggregating across all categories, the distribution was 100:24:22.

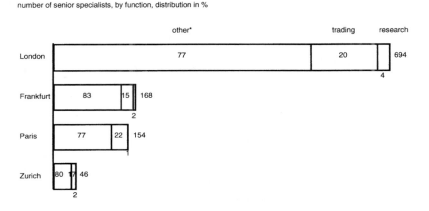

number of senior specialists, by function, distribution in %

*   not specified (may contain trading and research)
Source: Euromoney Bank Register

Figure 2.7   Forex trading, research and other functions, 1998

Cross-border Lending

It could be argued that cross-border and syndicated lending is not normally considered to be part of investment banking, since the latter is concerned with market-centred transactions, and not the provision of credit. It is included here nonetheless because cross-border and syndicated lending shares many of the characteristics of other markets discussed in this section. It is driven by the skills of the people doing the deal, rather than a retail presence or access to a local banking licence. Indeed, many of the necessary skills are very similar to those necessary to underwrite fixed-income products. Also, some of syndicated lending found in our statistics represents an integral part of a business transaction that is fully investment-banking driven in nature, such as the syndicated loan to the Olivetti subsidiary during the firm's takeover of Telecom Italia, which was later followed by a euro 6 bn Eurobond.

Data availability is good for cross-border lending. Concentration in cross-border lending has increased in recent years: the share of total volume taken by the top five countries rose from 75 per cent to 88 per cent between 1996 and 1998. The UK in particular had marked gains in market share, winning an extra 6 per cent of business. Germany, the US and Switzerland also raised their share of the total pie by 1–3 percentage points, while France

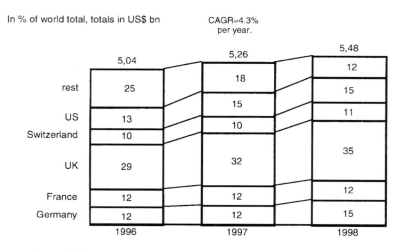

Source: BIS

Figure 2.8   Cross-border lending, 1996–8

stagnated. The primary result was a reduction in the market share of remaining countries (Figure 2.8).

Senior staff figures are broadly in line, although we only have information on syndicated lending, thereby reducing the likelihood of finding an exact parallel with the figures presented above. London had a little less than 5 times the senior syndicated lending staff at Frankfurt had, and 8.4 times that of Paris.

Over-the-counter Derivatives Trading

Over-the-counter (OTC) derivatives trading has increased substantially over the past few years. According to the International Securities Dealers Association (ISDA), notional amounts outstanding grew at an average annual rate of 43 per cent between 1993 and 1998. In 1998 alone, there was an increase of 75 per cent in the notional value of interest-rate swaps, currency swaps and interest-rate options. The adverse effects of the emerging-market crisis in 1998 therefore did not lead to a reduction in overall OTC activity.

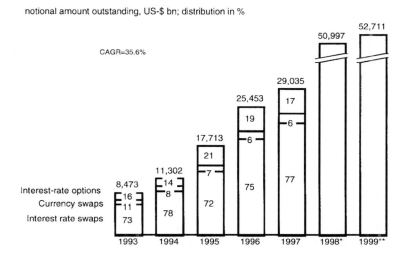

notional amount outstanding, US-$ bn; distribution in %

* No disaggregated figures available
** End of first half of 1999
Source: BIS 69th Annual Report, p. 132

Figure 2.9   OTC derivatives, 1993–8

The increase in traded volumes has been somewhat slower. Between 1995 and 1998 alone, average daily trading (in terms of notional amounts) grew by 76 per cent, from US$270 bn to US$474 bn. Incidentally, this suggests that the ratio of the value of OTC derivatives trades to total value outstanding declined rather sharply, from a factor of 3.4 to 2, over the same period.[15] Annual growth was even faster than in forex trading, with a cumulative average growth of 20.6 per cent per year compared with 15.5 per cent per year. Most of the growth could be accounted for by the rapid increase in currency-swap and options activity, as well the growth in interest-rate swaps. In contrast, floating rate notes (FRAs) have shown much slower rates of growth.

There has also been a significant trend towards greater concentration in the trading of OTC derivatives in the period 1995–8. The share of the top three countries increased from 59 per cent to 65 per cent of the total. The largest centre continued to be the UK, followed by the US. The UK increased its share very substantially, gaining 9 percentage points over six years. While it was ahead of its nearest competitor by 7 per cent in 1992, the differential became a much more commanding 17 per cent by 1998. There was a change in third place between 1995 and 1998. Japan commanded a 12 per cent share of global OTC derivatives activity in 1995, 4 per cent ahead of France, but it had fallen to fourth place in 1998, marginally behind France. Singapore had one of the quickest falls in market share over the period (of 38 per cent), while Germany gained substantially, but from a low base (Figure 2.11). Overall volume in percentage terms grew most rapidly in Germany, which

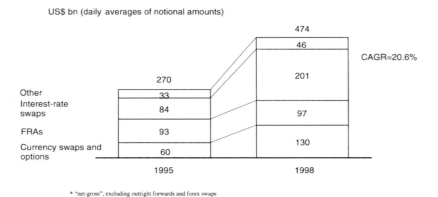

US$ bn (daily averages of notional amounts)

* "net-gross", excluding outright forwards and forex swaps
Source: BIS

Figure 2.10   Global turnover in OTC derivatives,* 1995 and 1998

In % of total turnover, totals in US$ bn

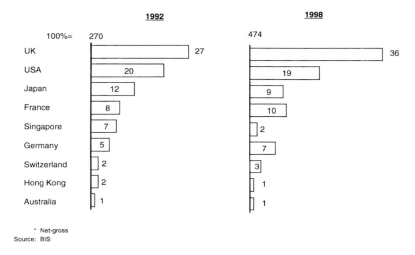

Figure 2.11   Shares in total OTC derivatives trading,* 1992 and 1998

In %, totals in US$ bn

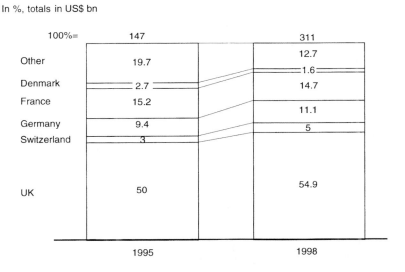

Figure 2.12   Market share of selected countries in OTC derivatives trading in Europe, 1995 and 1998

recorded an increase of 149 per cent over these three years, followed by the UK (131 per cent gain) and France (105 per cent gain).

Thus, the main European centres have managed to gain in relation to total global volume. How has this increase been divided up within Europe? In 1998 the City's commanding lead also continued to grow, with its market share increasing from 50 per cent to 54.9 per cent. Germany achieved a position only slightly behind that of France, having captured 11.1 per cent of the market, a gain of 1.7 percentage points. France, by contrast, lost 0.5 a percentage point of market share, and ended up with only 14.7 per cent of the European total (Figure 2.12).

There is one important new product in the OTC range: credit derivatives. Volumes outstanding are still small, but they are growing at a brisk pace. Compared with the (already optimistic) expectations of a few years ago, growth rates have been stunning. By the end of 1998, according to estimates compiled by the British Bankers' Association (BBA), the market was already bigger than most participants asked in 1996 had expected it to be by the end of the century. Many players in the industry believe it to be an area of strategic importance. In the early stages of the Asian crisis, the market was buoyed by a greater inclination to buy credit risk protection, and 62 per cent of the leading houses surveyed by the BBA reported that activity increased in response to the meltdown in Asia, and none saw a fall in activity.[16] 1998, however, marked a possible turning point, as default swaps written against emerging-market debt caused considerable legal difficulties. Documentation turned out to be ambiguous; credit events were

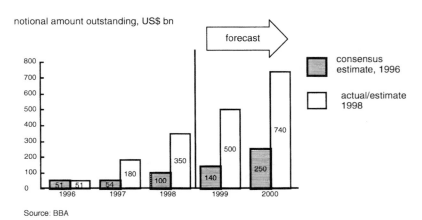

Source: BBA

Figure 2.13   Development of credit derivatives, actual and estimate, 1996–2000

hard to define in an impartial way.[17] Volume in 1999 slumped because of these difficulties.[18] The ISDA is now trying to remedy these problems by introducing new, standardized contracts. This will help to avoid uncertainty of the kind that surrounded, for example, Credit Suisse First Boston's (CSFB) dealings in the Russian market.[19]

Assessing the strength in new product areas such as this one requires survey methods, as normal statistical sources are not yet unavailable. The BBA's surveys suggest that London, together with New York, is the leading financial centre for credit derivatives. Although invented in the US, London's easier regulatory regime has made it a congenial place for the market to grow and mature. Even if the BBA's results have to be taken with a pinch of salt, it is telling that 80 per cent of market participants assume that London will be more important than New York as a centre for credit derivatives activity by the year 2000. Expert projections are that its market share will rise from 39 per cent in 1997 to 49 per cent in 1998, and 51 per cent in 2000.

The source of that strength is particularly apparent in the market for credit derivatives written against underlyings from the East Asia, where London dominates the business. Of the 18 leading houses surveyed by the BBA, ten booked all their credit derivatives business in London, and four booked all their European and Asian transactions there. The City's light regulations did much to move the market from its origins in New York across the Atlantic.[20] Also, the Financial Services Authority (FSA) took an early lead in ensuring that credit derivatives could be used to reduce the amount of risk capital required for the loan book (where the adjustment is, however, small) and in the trading book (where perfect hedges could be used for a full offset). The FSA's rules from 22 July 1998, ahead of the Basle revisions, did much to reassure market participants of continuing favourable treatment.[21]

The market's development on the continent has been markedly slower. For instance, industry participants have complained about the German regulator, the Bundesaufsichtsamt für das Kreditwesen (BAKred), for insisting on somewhat lengthy approval procedures. Bayerische Landesbank spent months applying and receiving regulatory approval for its entry into the credit derivatives market.[22] Also many banks are state-owned or co-operatives, and are less subject to the same pressures for cost-efficiency and higher returns as their Anglo-Saxon rivals, reducing the need to improve returns and thereby making it harder to establish strong domestic demand for credit derivatives in these markets.

Fixed-income Trading

The location of bond trading is hard to determine, as the business always used to be conducted almost exclusively over the telephone. In recent months, however, Euro MTS, a trading system originally developed for Italian government securities, has begun to make inroads, thus reducing the preponderance of OTC trading. However, trading volumes by location can still only be properly reconstructed with the data from the large clearing organizations (which appear to be unable or unwilling to share them). Instead, therefore, the focus will be on the number of senior staff by function.

In 1998, London's lead was particularly large in trading and sales. More than 80 per cent of all traders are located there, and 78 per cent in fixed-income sales. Interestingly, fixed income trading is one of the few areas in which Paris actually attracts a larger number of staff than Frankfurt – but the same is not true of sales. Industry experts explain Paris's lead by its use of the primary government bond dealer system, which imposes more stringent residence requirements on dealers. Where the specialization of staff is not broken down further (and hence is likely to contain some

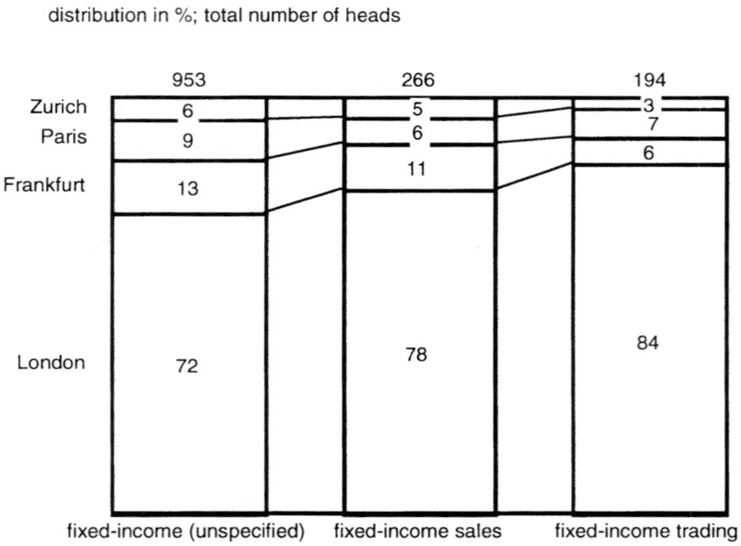

distribution in %; total number of heads

Source: Euromoney Bank Register

Figure 2.14   Senior staff in fixed-income trading and sales, 1998

issuance, and so on), the lead is somewhat smaller. Also, Frankfurt is ahead of Paris by a comfortable margin in both sales and the unspecified group. It therefore appears that Paris's unusually good showing in terms of fixed income issuance owes more to protectionist measures than to the competitiveness of it as an international financial centre.

Findings in this section also cast some light on the shackles with which governments that try to support their financial centres need to contend. The battle for the benchmark in Euroland, for instance, was aired in the press for a long time. Using the considerably more efficient primary government bond dealer system, and issuing continuously along the whole yield curve to ensure liquidity, the French government made a conscious effort to attain benchmark status for its obligations assimilable du trésor (OATs). Ultimately, at the long end of the curve, the German Bund contract won – not through sophistication or skill, but sheer size, some would argue. At the shorter end of the yield curve, however, French bonds are often more liquid, due to a more efficient repo market. Also, 30-year OATs tend to trade below Bunds.[23] Approximately one-third of new issues in euros is priced over OATs, and two-thirds over Bunds. Internally, and for hedging, the swap curve is frequently used.[24] As is true in most products that require next to no face-to-face contact or physical presence, the location of value-added activities is hardly influenced at all by this. This is not to say that benchmark status is not a prize worth having, since it also entails lower funding costs for the government, for example. Nonetheless, in terms of the standing of its prime financial centre, Germany's success has managed to retain lustre for it but it has not gained in employment statistics or competitiveness.

Summary: For a Few Dollars More

In the global product area, successes for the continental financial centres are few and far between. Germany has seen spectacular growth in OTC derivatives, and scored a symbolic victory by establishing its Bunds as the Euro benchmark at the long end of the yield curve. In cross-border lending, both Germany and the UK are gaining market share rapidly, while France appears to be stagnating. In most of these products, the impact on the bottom line for these financial centres is rather sparse. Spreads are very small, and total revenues in, for example, forex trading, were estimated at approximately US$10 bn in 1996, less than one-third of the revenues generated by equity IPOs in the US alone in the same year.[25]

INFRASTRUCTURE-DRIVEN PRODUCTS

To distinguish between truly globalized and infrastructure-driven products is to invite criticism. This is because of the momentous changes that have occurred in the latter product category in recent years. Technology has transformed the way exchanges operate, clearing and settlement are conducted and custody is organized.

Exchange-traded Derivatives

Exchange-traded products used to be strongly tied to one physical location. The gradual demise of the pit and the rise of electronic trading systems have changed all this. Most prominently amongst them, derivatives have moved off the floor and over to screen-based trading systems. Eurex, the German-Swiss alliance, the exchange that pioneered electronic trading, has almost as many members outside the founding countries as in them, with 149 members out of a total of 313 coming from 13 countries other than Switzerland or Germany. Overall growth in market size has been healthy,

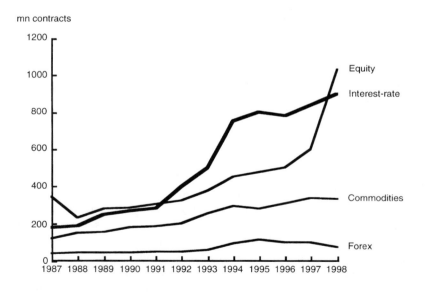

Source: Systematics International

Figure 2.15   Number of exchange-traded derivatives contracts, 1987–98

with the number of contracts being traded growing by 10.7 per cent per year between 1995 and 1998.

Interest-rate contracts and equity contracts account for about 40 per cent each of the total of traded contracts. 1998 was the first year since 1991 that equity-based products recorded a higher number of transactions than interest-based instruments. This tallies with the finding that the size of equity markets is catching up fast with global debt markets. Currency derivatives trading has declined somewhat in absolute value in recent years, whereas commodities trading has shown healthy growth.

Annual number of contracts, mn

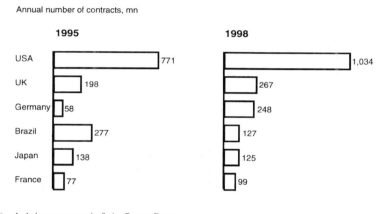

*   Includes turnover on the Swiss-German Eurex
Source: Systematics International

Figure 2.16   Location of international exchange-traded derivatives turnover, 1995 and 1998

Unlike the products described above, growth in volume has not gone hand in hand with increased concentration. Concentration in exchange trading of derivatives has actually declined in recent years, with the share of the top three countries falling from 75 per cent to 68 per cent. One area in particular has seen the impact of electronic systems: the trading of long-dated interest rate contracts. Rates of growth in the number of contracts traded show the outstanding performance of Germany. Admittedly starting from a low base, it managed to grow some 328 per cent in the three years 1995–8, nearly ten times as much as the performances of the UK and US, leaving the UK only a nose ahead in the race for second place in terms of total market share. France also moved forward; relative to its competitors, however, it only just ambled off the starting line. Germany's success is

Page

epitomized by the changes that have occurred in the trading of long-dated interest-rate contracts, where Eurex stole a march on the London International Financial Futures Exchange (LIFFE) by capturing all of the trading in the world's largest financial contract, the Bund future.

Focusing on individual exchanges instead of countries, recent trends show the dire straits that LIFFE increasingly finds itself in. In the first half of 1999, Eurex was the world's most active derivatives exchange. In the same period, LIFFE lost almost 40 per cent of its trading volume. Whether the number of contracts traded or their value is the best measure for exchange performance can be debated. For instance, much of the improvement in Matif/Monep's equity turnover is a result of reducing contract size from 100 shares to 10. LIFFE lost almost nothing in terms of the value of traded contracts.

* Matif/Monep not included due to a change in counting methodology
Source: FOW TradeData

Figure 2.17 Derivatives exchanges' volumes, 1998–9

Eurex's strength is largely underpinned by the success of the euro Bund contract. Following 95 per cent growth between the first half of 1998 and the first half of 1999, it is the most actively traded futures contract in the world. The DAX contract and the euro Bobl are also strong performers, but in the short-term interest-rate segment, LIFFE's Euribor contract continues to dominate. Partly because of changes in the specification, Matif/Monep's

number of contracts traded, mn

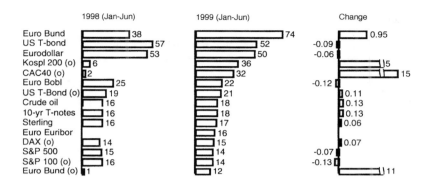

Source: FOW TradeData

Figure 2.18   Contract volumes, 1998–9

option on the CAC40 has seen the highest growth of all derivatives traded on exchanges, followed by the option on the euro Bund.

In short-term interest-rate products, LIFFE continues to dominate. Its Euribor contract accounts for approximately 90 per cent of short euro-interest rate futures in Europe, with Eurex and Matif sharing the remaining 10 per cent. Germany is well-positioned in the trading of equity derivatives, the fastest-growing area of exchange-based derivatives trading (Table 2.1). The option on the DAX has captured 10 per cent of the global market for equity index derivatives, ahead of all continental rivals, and with twice the market share of the CAC40, or 2.5 times that of the FTSE 100.

Nor is growth of a more integrated European capital market doing much to undermine this position. The Dow-Jones Euro-Stoxx 50 is by far the most successful of the new pan-European equity indices. In the first half of 1999, some 1,910,000 futures contracts were traded, more than 30 times the 54,950 futures contracts on the FTSE Eurotop 100 index traded on LIFFE/AEX.[26]

It should first be noted that it is difficult to separate out OTC and exchange-traded derivatives staff. In 1998, there were 738 senior derivatives specialists in London, Frankfurt, Paris and Zurich. Of these, 66 per cent are located in London, a little less than 15 per cent in Frankfurt and 11 per cent in Paris. Zurich has 8 per cent of the total. These proportions vary somewhat by product category. In equity derivatives, London's strength is above average, with 73 per cent of all specialists working in that field, as against 12 per cent in Frankfurt and only 7 per cent in Paris. In fixed-income, however, London's position is markedly weaker, and Frankfurt can claim almost one-fifth of the pie (Table 2.2).

Table 2.1   Equity index derivatives: turnover, 1998

Index	Volume, US$ mn	% share
S&P 500	60.5	55.5
DAX	11.2	10.3
Nikkei 225	8.2	7.5
CAC40	6.6	6.1
MIB 30	5.5	5.0
FTSE 100	4.5	4.1
AEX	3.1	2.8
IBEX 35	2.4	2.2
SMI	2.3	2.1
Hang Seng	1.8	1.7
Other	3.1	2.8
Total	109.2	100.0

Source: Goldman Sachs

Table 2.2   Senior derivatives staff by location and speciality, 1998

	Derivatives total	Derivatives (unspecified)	Fixed-income derivatives	Equity derivatives
Number of staff				
London	493	376	43	74
Frankfurt	107	80	15	12
Paris	80	63	10	7
Zurich	58	36	13	9
Total	738	555	81	102
Percentage of total				
London	67	68	53	72
Frankfurt	14	15	19	12
Paris	11	11	12	7
Zurich	8	6	16	9

Source: Euromoney Bank Register

Clearing and Settlement

In principle, clearing and settlement can also be conducted from any location that offers access – direct or remote – to the national or international clearing organizations like Sicovam, Cedel or Euroclear, as well as a good communications infrastructure and skilled personnel. Cost pressures strongly favour concentrating these operations, which can easily be physically separate from trading rooms, and so on, in one location. Frankfurt is widely seen as well-positioned here. Partly for cultural reasons, streamlining factory-style operations, minimizing the likelihood of errors and making economies of scale appear to be easier in the country of Xetra and Deutsche Terminbörse (DTB). Of all heads of settlement, 23 per cent are located in Frankfurt (substantially higher than the 14 per cent in all functions), compared with 69 per cent in London and 8 per cent in Paris. The big push for concentration may still be to come. In many back offices, coping with the introduction of the euro and the Y2K (Year 2000) problem has meant that reorganizations have been put on hold. It may well be that, come 2000, many more securities firms will decide to consolidate their back offices in one location.

Equity Trading

Estimating equity trading volumes by location is notoriously difficult. A scholar recently working on the issue spoke of 'lies, damned lies, and turnover statistics'[27] because of national differences in the way turnover is counted. Second, due to the rise of electronic trading, turnover statistics by exchange only tell us so much about the location of the traders, since increasingly members transact from locations elsewhere. At the end of 1998, for example, the German Stock Exchange had 38 members in eight countries outside Germany.

This is not the first time that this issue has been confronted, and we have to rely on figures compiled by the World Bank. These do, however, solve the most pressing problems of double counting and of defining the type of transaction being counting (adjusting differences in terms of two schools of thought – the trading system views as against the regulated environment view).[28]

Within what is today the EMU area, concentration of share trading has not increased, in contrast to common belief. Whereas, in 1990, the top two stock exchanges in what was to become the euro area traded 83 times the number of equities of the bottom two, this figure had fallen to 27 by 1998. The reduction in inequality was also true more generally. If we use the Gini coefficient as a measure of equality, there is a sharp downward movement – falling from 0.45 to 0.3, a considerable change in less than a decade.[29]

Of course, the effect of the euro is not yet reflected in the Lorenz curves in Figure 2.19. However, given that real and monetary economic convergence in the run-up to EMU was substantial, we believe there is little

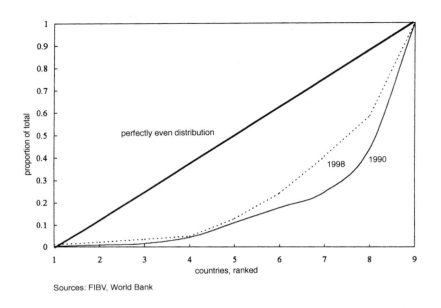

Sources: FIBV, World Bank

Figure 2.19   Lorenz curves, stock-exchange trading in Europe, 1990 and 1998

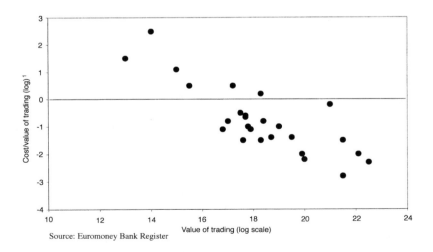

Source: Euromoney Bank Register

Figure 2.20   Costs and scale of stock exchanges

reason for the recent trend to be reversed in the near future. This finding is puzzling. Simple intuition as well as the empirical evidence strongly suggest that there should be considerable economies of scale in trading equities, since the fixed costs for an electronic system (or a floor) are substantial, and marginal costs are not. Recent research confirms that cost-efficiency rises rapidly with total volume.

The cost-efficiency of stock exchanges continues to vary widely. In 1999, the Bank of Finland conducted a comparative study of overall cost efficiency, using the latest available set of published accounts. The author's method was to regress total cost on trading volume and the number of firms listed, as well as a set of control variables. The residuals of this regression are therefore the unexplained part of cost variation, that is, indicative of cost performance relative to other exchanges, adjusted for economies of scale and other factors.[30] Figure 2.21 gives the main results.

In 1997 the New Year Stock Exchange (NYSE) was by far the most cost-efficient stock exchange in the sample; the AMEX and Tokyo come at the bottom of the list. Of the three main continental rivals, Germany scored best, followed by London and then, at some distance, Paris. Note, however, that the efficiency model underlying the Bank of Helsinki ranking did not take *more than proportional* cost reduction as a result of economies of scale into account, which may be substantial. Hence, efficiency comparisons are only strictly valid for exchanges with similar turnover.

residuals of regression (dep. var.: cost, explanatory variables: size, joint platform)

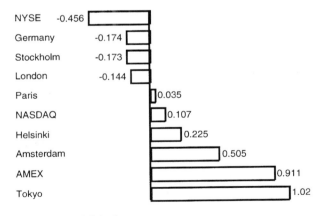

Source: Bank of Finland

Figure 2.21 Relative cost-efficiency of stock exchanges, 1997

The year 1998 was a good one for most exchanges, with increases in trading volume partly driven by the strength of equity markets. In terms of year-on-year growth, Germany topped the table in 1998, with the value of shares traded surging ahead by almost half. The UK was second with 43 per cent, followed by the Netherlands and France. London continued to be the largest exchange in the time zone in terms of total value of traded shares. Its dominance in trading international equities was the driving factor, contributing almost half of the total turnover.

The cost-efficiency of stock exchanges can also be compared by examining the share of trading 'lost' to the world's largest exchange, the NYSE. Firms seeking a listing outside their home market are not necessarily signalling dissatisfaction with their home exchange. This is because a US listing is tantamount to a rubber seal of approval, making it easier to attract investors and raising a company's international profile. The decisive question is how much of the trading actually shifts once a cross-listing has occurred. Some of the exchanges that are struggling, such as Toronto, have seen much of their volume migrate to New York: NYSE volumes in Canadian stocks were equivalent to 24 per cent of Toronto's in 1998.[31]

In the case of the three countries mainly considered in this book, there is no dramatic leaking away of liquidity on this scale. However, it is interesting to note the differences in the extent to which US investors, especially the big institutions, seem to switch trading to the NYSE once there is a dual listing: a rather circuitous but all the same telling way of

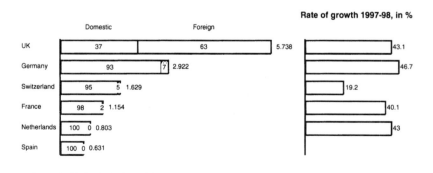

Sources: World Bank, national exchanges, FIBV

Figure 2.22   Equity trading volume by country (US$mn), 1997/8 (distribution in %)

comparing stock exchanges' efficiency. Germany has lost the smallest share of total trading to the NYSE. Less than 1 per cent of firms listed there also trade on the Big Board; the share of trading 'lost' is actually even lower than that, at 0.7 per cent. The UK has experienced more dual listings, and trading has migrated across the Atlantic: some 3 per cent of trades in UK shares now occur at the NYSE. Interestingly, it is the large, high-volume shares that have migrated disproportionately. A similar picture can be observed in France, which has suffered the highest 'loss' of trading volume. Almost 4 per cent of turnover (by value) is now in New York, while only 2 per cent of firms are listed there. Overall, these shifts in the locus of trading suggest that the efficiency ranking provided by the Bank of Finland is spot-on. The least efficient bourse in our sample has lost the greatest share of trading, while the most efficient has seen next to no volume migrate across the Atlantic.

In equity trading, London attracts more than its average share of staff (according to the Euromoney Bank Register). In sales, which is closely linked in terms of processes and people, the proportions are similar, at 81 per cent in London, compared with 9 per cent in Frankfurt and 7 per cent in Paris (with the remainder in Zurich). Where only a general category for equity is given in the Euromoney Bank Register, the respective figures are 75 per cent, 13 per cent and 8 per cent.

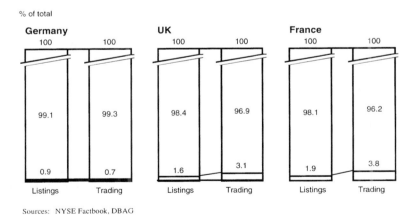

Sources: NYSE Factbook, DBAG

Figure 2.23   Distribution of listings and trading volume (by value), NYSE compared with home country

Summary

Success has come quickly to the centres that adopted the electronic technologies for trading derivatives and stocks early. Eurex's gains at the expense of LIFFE are one example. It goes from strength to strength, overtaking even the Chicago Board of Trade (CBOT) in terms of the number of contracts traded in the first half of 1999.[32] Given the flying start that Eurex had in the US after the recent change of heart at the Commodities Futures Trade Commission (CFTC) about the use of foreign terminals, this trend is likely to continue. Also, the stock exchanges that appear to hold up best against the NYSE's attractions are the ones that have gone electronic.

For products with a strong infrastructure component, Germany appears to hold better cards than London. Thanks to the early, determined adoption of electronic trading systems, combined with a fully integrated stock exchange that offers derivatives and equity trading plus clearing and settlement, it is now amongst the world's most cost-efficient places to trade. At the same time, smaller stock exchanges such as Vienna and Helsinki are beginning to adopt the German Xetra system and use the Frankfurt infrastructure directly.

Paris, despite its early adoption of electronic trading, appears to lag behind. Its efficiency is not impressive, according to the Bank of Finland, and the Paris Bourse has lost more trading to the NYSE than the exchanges in Frankfurt and London. In derivatives trading, it appears to lack critical mass. Attempts to establish OATs as a benchmark in Europe, and with that to win the majority of trading in long-dated government bond futures, have gone nowhere.

It is for similar reasons that continental centres have not gained a greater share of specialized staff. Remote membership and clearing have allowed the major players to make decisions about location without giving too much thought to the quality of the domestic infrastructure.

'STICKY' PRODUCTS

In the final category in this section, the products contain a larger local component – they are 'sticky' in the sense that the provision of the service is not very mobile. The extent to which these services have to be provided domestically varies. However, from asset management to M&A, there are important similarities. Origination staff is very often local, and often comprises a high number of senior specialists. Execution staff need much less local contact, and are often placed in 'hubs' or work in a few 'factories' world-wide.

Asset Management

Asset management is often considered to be one of the most attractive areas of wholesale banking. Stable fee and commission earnings and an increasing proportion of assets managed by institutions make this business a priority for many securities firms. In addition to sizeable inflows, good returns in most of the world's equity and bond markets have driven up the value of funds under management. In Europe, the value of assets managed by institutional investors has grown at an annual rate of 14 per cent in the period 1990–8. Perhaps even more importantly, disintermediation has only just begun in earnest in Europe, leading to an increasing switch of customers out of bank deposits into capital-market instruments, often administered by institutional investors. Finally, the inevitable crisis of old-age pension systems will lead to very considerable inflows.

Assets under management in the UK have grown less fast than in Europe overall in the 1990s, increasing at 13.5 per cent per year, whereas Germany has surged ahead at a rate of 17.2 per cent. France has lagged behind substantially, recording growth of only 10.7 per cent. Despite this slow growth, the UK remains by far the largest centre for institutional asset management services; relative to GDP, the amount of assets under management is second only to the US. The absolute amount is also approximately 70 per cent higher than in Germany or France (Figure 2.24).

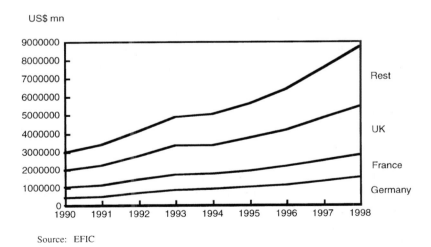

Source: EFIC

Figure 2.24   Assets under institutional management, 1990–8

distribution of investors' assets, %

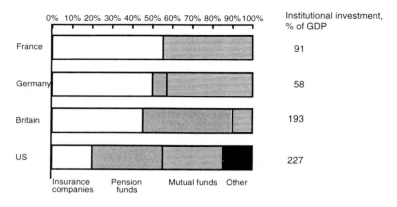

Source: OECD

Figure 2.25   Financial assets of institutional investors, 1997

The proportion of equity holdings to total funds varies considerably more than the totals under management. A very high proportion, around two thirds, of all the funds held by UK asset managers are in equities, compared with 13 per cent in Germany and 22 per cent in France. Thus, in this particularly profitable and dynamic subsector, the UK leads the world in value of holdings, and Tokyo's earlier leading position has suffered from weakness in the Japanese markets.[33] As Figure 2.26 shows, London has spectacularly increased its position in managing institutional equity holdings. It has dethroned Tokyo as the world's leading centre for equity fund management, and has pulled further ahead of New York. Zurich has continued to defend its position as the second-largest centre for equity fund management in Europe, with Geneva, Paris and Frankfurt trailing at a respectable distance. Paris and Frankfurt have increased the value under management slightly. The presence of centres like Boston, San Francisco and Edinburgh also highlights the importance of lifestyle considerations in attracting talented staff – today, remote membership and the quality of telecommunications may be sufficient to compensate for the disadvantages of not being in one of the traditional centres provided that staff is scarce, and sufficiently charmed by the urban area in question.

In terms of the number of staff, the UK appears to lead by a margin considerably larger than can be explained by differences in assets under management (Table 2.3). Although total assets managed by institutions are about 70 per cent larger in the UK than in the Germany or France, London

in US$ 000's bn

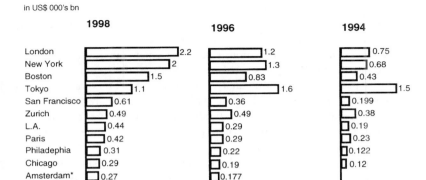

Figure 2.26   Institutional equity holdings, 1994, 1996 and 1998

absolute numbers; productivity = volume managed per portfolio manager, US$ bn

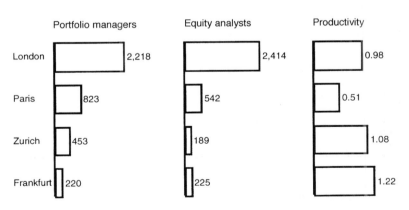

Source: Technimetrics

Figure 2.27   Equity portfolio managers and equity analysts, 1998

has four times the staff working in investment management of Paris or Zurich, and a full six times the staff levels in Frankfurt. One explanation is that London's core strength, equity fund management, generates not only the highest margins, but also significant employment opportunities. Figure 2.27 confirms this hypothesis.[34] London leads in the number of equity portfolio managers and equity analysts by a substantial margin of approximately 10:1 compared with Frankfurt, and 3:1 compared with Paris. Overall productivity, measured as funds under management per portfolio manager, is close to 1 bn everywhere except for Paris, which lags behind by approximately 50 per cent.

To include private banking under the heading of asset management is a question of definition. In more ways than one, it shares many of the same core skills; what differs primarily is the distribution channel used. In private banking, London's lead is somewhat less commanding. This is largely because Zurich remains a centre of private banking activity, attracting some 28 per cent of senior staff in the field. Despite lacking the obvious advantages of Switzerland with its the tax benefits it offers and continuing opportunities to obscure ownership, London has the highest number of senior private banking staff in Europe.

Table 2.3   Senior staff in private banking and investment management, 1998

	Private banking	Investment management
Number of staff		
London	43	103
Frankfurt	18	16
Paris	25	25
Zurich	34	27
Total	120	171
Percentage of total		
London	36	60
Frankfurt	15	9
Paris	21	15
Zurich	28	16

Source: Bank of Finland

Finally, principal investment may also be considered under the heading of asset management. In the case of 'blind pool' participations (where investors contribute funds that are not tied to one specific project), the overall structure is fairly similar to closed-end mutual funds or unit trusts. However, the degree of management intervention that an investment entails is often even higher than in the case of the most active mutual funds. Often,

years of close co-operation with the management are needed to turn a
company around – and sell it subsequently. This increases the local
component and makes the product even more sticky, that is, it requires more
face-to-face interaction as well as an intimate understanding of cultures and
preferences.

Fixed-income Issuance

The total volume of bonds issued has grown considerably over the last few
years. Here, we disregard sovereign issuance – which only offers very slim
pickings for investment banks. Instead, we focus on issuance of non-
sovereigns as a prime source of earnings in this area. Figure 2.28 gives an
overview of total investment-grade non-US issuance from 1990 to 1998.
Totals have grown at an average annual growth rate of 26 per cent per year.

European firms and institutions have continued to be active in this
market. Eurobonds have been of particular interest. Germany has been the
largest issuer not only in a European context, but world-wide (disregard-
ing the special position of supranationals such as the World Bank). It was
only in 1998 that the US drew level in terms of issuance in the Eurobond
market. Between 1994 and 1998, Germany's slice of the pie shrunk
somewhat, not because of lower issuance, but because growth for other
issuers was faster. France shrunk by almost half in terms of total market
share, falling from 9 per cent in 1994 to 5 per cent in 1998. The UK had
its ups and downs, but gained 3 percentage points between 1994 and 1998
in total.

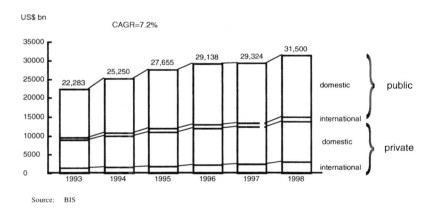

Figure 2.28   Total global debt, volume outstanding: market split, 1990–8

distribution %, totals US$ bn

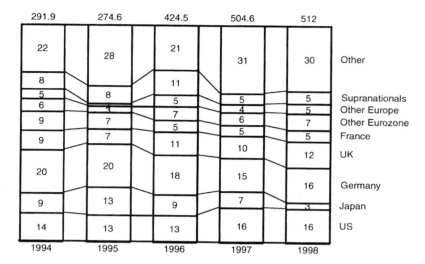

Source: IFR Platinum

Figure 2.29   Eurobond issuance: issuer split, 1994–8

In recent years the European high-yield market has begun to take off. Between 1994 and 1998, the value of new issuance increased tenfold, with the number of new issues reaching the market growing by a factor of 8. Average margins actually increased, from 180 basis points (bp) in 1994 to 300 in 1997, before declining slightly to 275 in 1998. They were therefore approximately twice the level in the US.[35] Despite the value of US-issuance being 16 times that in Europe, the size of the total revenue pool only differed by a factor of 9.[36]

In the period 1994–8, the UK contributed 64 per cent to the total, with Germany at 4 per cent and France 5 per cent. 1999 may well be a turning point for the market as a whole. European issuance in the first quarter was US$5.6 bn, and the figure for the full year may well reach US$20 bn.[37]

Asset-backed issuance has grown markedly in the last few years. Between 1994 and 1997, the value of all asset-backed securities (ABS) bonds issued by French, German or UK borrowers increased more than tenfold, before declining somewhat in 1998. Due to the limited absolute size of the market and the low number of total issues, market share continued to fluctuate wildly from one year to the next. In all years save one, France was a larger issuer than Germany, and the UK recorded the

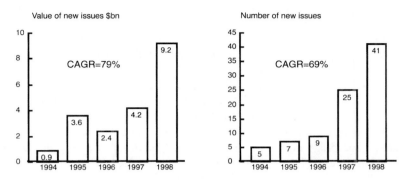

Sources: IFR Platinum, McKinsey

Figure 2.30   High-yield issuance in Europe, 1994–8

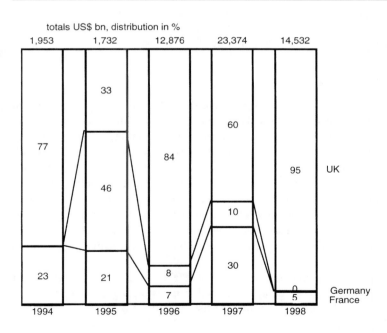

Source: IFR Platinum

Figure 2.31   ABS issuance in Germany, UK and France, 1994–8

one, France was a larger issuer than Germany, and the UK recorded the highest volume in all years except 1995.

In mortgage-backed bonds, the volume of issuance between 1994 and 1998 leapt by 137 per cent in the three main countries in this book. Issuance was actually strongest from Scandinavian institutions first; it is only recently that other countries have begun to catch up. In 1998, German issuance at US$1,570 mn was slightly behind the French with US$1,916 mn, with the UK ahead with a total volume of US$6,543 mn.

However, comparisons based on mortgage-backed securities (MBS) only are inappropriate in the case of Germany. *Pfandbriefe* are very similar to MBS deals, except that the loans remain on the book of the issuing bank and are also highly cost-efficient (they are also highly attractive because they require less capital under German rules). If *Pfandbriefe* are included, Germany easily leads in this market segment. Volume is extremely high – the total value of outstanding German *Pfandbriefe* in 1998 was higher than the value of all public debt in any one European country.[38] In recent years, a trend towards 'Jumbo' issues has increased liquidity and the quality of prices dramatically, and the listing of a Jumbo-future allows efficient trading and risk-management. Since their launch in 1995, Jumbos have gained 22 per cent of the total market.[39]

Equity Issuance

In the last few years the value of world equity markets has grown much more rapidly than that of bond markets. Annual growth rates between 1993 and 1998 were almost double the levels in bond markets, at 13 per cent per year instead of 7 per cent per year. On present trends, equity markets will overtake bond markets in terms of absolute size within a few years.[40] Gains in market size are the result of two main factors: higher valuation levels for existing firms, and new listings. In the recent past, changes in the former were far more important than changes in the latter. A recent wave of privatizations and demutualizations across Europe, combined with a set of new markets specifically designed for young high-growth firms, has begun to change this.

The number of domestic listings in the UK continues to be notably larger than in the two continental financial centres combined. But while in Germany and France the number of listings have grown by an average of 13.8 and 6.9 per cent per year, respectively, the UK has actually experienced a decline by 11.6 per cent in 1998.

Within Europe, most markets have seen quite high levels of equity issuance in the last few years. In 1998 the UK continued to dominate in

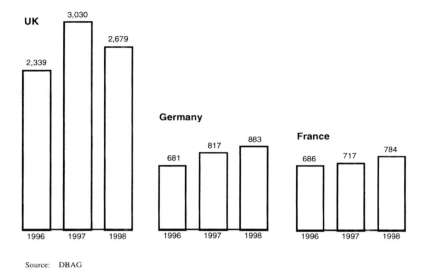

Source: DBAG

Figure 2.32 Number of quoted domestic companies, 1996–8

terms of total issuance, followed by France and Germany. Despite buoyant
equity markets, however, the 1994 peak in equity issuance was not regained
in all markets. In almost all European countries, seasoned equity offerings
have dominated issuance (Figure 2.33). The only notable exceptions can
be observed when privatizations temporarily drive up the volume of IPOs.
In general, the structure is closer to balance in the UK than on the continent.

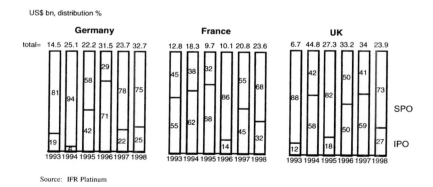

Source: IFR Platinum

Figure 2.33 Equity issuance in Germany, France and the UK, 1993–8

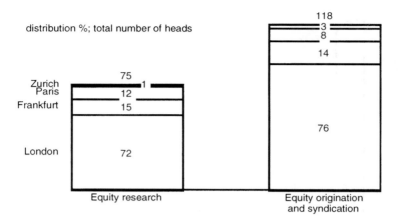

Source: Euromoney Bank Register

Figure 2.34   Senior staff in equity research and origination/syndication, 1998

For all their success in attracting more listings recently, Paris and London still only have a fairly small number of staff dedicated to equity origination/syndication. London has 72 per cent of the senior staff in the four leading European centres, with Frankfurt at 15 per cent and Paris 12 per cent of the total. The picture is similar to the one in equity research, where London has 72 per cent of the total.

Mergers and Acquisitions

M&A activity world-wide has increased dramatically since 1990 (Figure 2.35). The total value of all transactions world-wide has grown of an annual rate of 20 per cent, quadrupling since the beginning of the 1990s. Remarkably, the most advanced market in 1990, the US, has continued to dominate. This is despite the fact that many industry observers would have expected catch-up growth in terms of the use of financial engineering, which should have narrowed the gap between the M&A volumes in the US and the rest. The share of all M&A deals done in the US has actually almost doubled, from 28.8 per cent in 1990 to 50.1 per cent in 1998.[41] A similar picture is seen in Europe, where the UK continues to be the largest market by far. The spectacular growth in France and Germany over the last few years has therefore not gained them a markedly higher proportion of the European M&A market; they have only slowly increased their share of the European total (Figure 2.36).

US$ bn

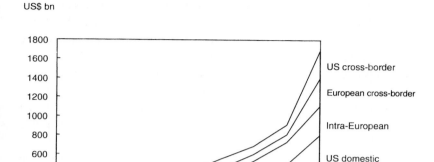

* Not adjusted for double-counting of European/US cross-border deals
Source: Securities Data Company

Figure 2.35   Global M&A transactions,* 1990–8

US$ mn; announcement date volumes

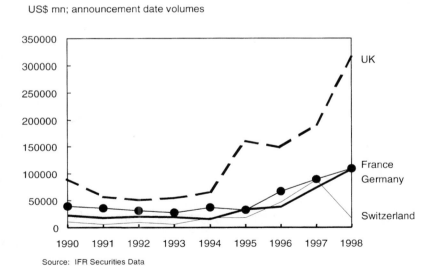

Source: IFR Securities Data

Figure 2.36   Size of M&A markets, 1990–8

Transactions volumes, however, are not the last word in terms of market attractiveness. Revenues vary more than fees since larger, more developed markets sustain lower margins. Estimates of fee levels are notoriously unreliable, but it appears that higher fees (up to 0.5 per cent in Germany and Italy) partly compensate for lower volumes. Depending on the estimates used, Germany may already be the largest market for M&A transactions in terms of total revenues. Figure 2.37. also shows two additional dimensions of market attractiveness: the cumulative average growth rate between 1990 and 1998, and absolute market size. Both in terms of total fees generated as well as growth rates, the German market appears more attractive than the French one. The UK has greater volumes, but lower revenues and slightly lower rates of growth. In the past, a considerable part of the growth in M&A volumes in Europe was driven by a higher proportion of transactions being done with the help of an adviser. Nearly all deals are now covered by M&A advisers (while, as recently as 1994, almost half of all German deals for example used no adviser), so that this source of growth is ruled out in the future. Instead, growth will mainly come from a greater number of deals, as well as greater value per deal.

growth rate %, revenue and market size, US$ mn

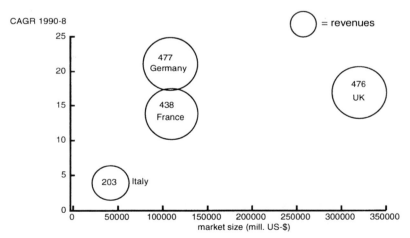

Source: McKinsey, IFR

Figure 2.37   M&A: market size, growth and revenues, 1998, estimate

US$ bn

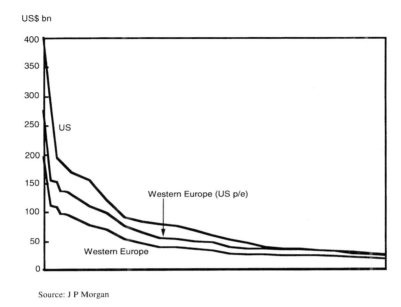

Source: J P Morgan

Figure 2.38   Market capitalization of top 100 firms, 28 April 1999

Total revenue appears to be a comprehensive measure of market attractiveness for intermediaries. Yet the revenues of intermediaries are the costs of clients, representing a real transfer from one part of the economy to another. Taking the difference between the fees in each continental market and those in the UK, we can calculate the size of this transfer. In the case of Germany, where fee levels are quite high, clients paid some US$170 mn in 1998 more than they would have done in the UK.[42] In France, the figure was an even more stunning US$202 mn. This, of course, does not approximate to a real burden on the economy; since clients paid these fees, they were (at least *ex ante*) convinced that they were receiving value for money. High fees are therefore just a form of capturing consumer rents. The extreme scarcity of good local staff who can do deals of world-class quality – another indicator of the necessarily 'sticky' nature of the business – is probably largely responsible for the current fee levels. The true welfare cost is best approximated by the number of transactions lost because of this; the higher fees simply reflect this fact.

If accelerated expansion and training of local workforces relieves this shortage – as it ultimately will – deal volume will surge. If the average relationship between deal volume and fee levels is any guide, a normalization

% of all deals

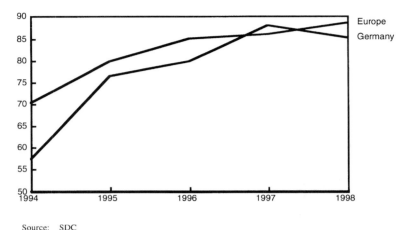

Source: SDC

Figure 2.39   Proportion of deals with adviser, 1994–8

of supply (and hence, a reduction of German fees to UK levels) should boost the size of the market to about US$330 bn per year. If the UK's ratio of deal size to GDP were reached, the figure could be as high as US$594 bn per year. For France, levels of between US$210 bn and US$370 bn appear possible. Note this is not a zero-sum game; since the response to changes in fee levels is considerable, the total size of the revenue pie for investment banks could still grow. At the same time, more services would be provided, thus enabling domestic firms on the continent to start competing more effectively. Concentration ratios in European M&A appear to be in line with those observed globally. While the top ten firms took 82 per cent of the market captured by the top 25 firms in global M&A, the ratio for Europe was 77 per cent.[43]

The distribution of staff can largely be explained by the size of domestic markets – but not quite. Although M&A volume in Germany and France is a little less than one-third that in the UK, the number of M&A specialists is only one-quarter (26 per cent for Frankfurt, 24 per cent for Paris). This suggests that London continues to play an important role as a hub from which to fly in execution specialists for the European deals, and that second-tier centres have been largely unsuccessful in growing into this role, primarily serving their domestic markets instead. Origination specialists, on the other hand, who maintain client relationships over long periods, almost always establish a national presence. As one investment banker put it, 'There is only room for one hub in each time zone, and in Europe, that's London.'[44] In part, London is beginning to widen its role even beyond that. This is underscored by the recent decision by Salomon Smith Barney, ranked sixth in the 1998 league table of M&A advisers by volume, to move their global acquisition finance group from New York to London. It thus follows a string of US buyout firms such as KKR that have set up shop in London.[45]

Buyouts

Much of the restructuring in the US that formed the basis for its present economic success was a result of the wave of buyouts in the 1980s. Buyouts have traditionally been much more common in the UK, and relatively rare on the continent. Over the years 1995–8, this has changed. Deal volumes in the UK have doubled, but the rate of increase on the continent has been at least as rapid. Germany experienced an increase in deal volumes by a factor of more than 3, and so did France.

Relative to the size of the economy, the Netherlands, Switzerland and Finland also record fairly high levels of activity, but absolute volumes are small. The growth in volume has been associated with a rise in the number

US$ bn

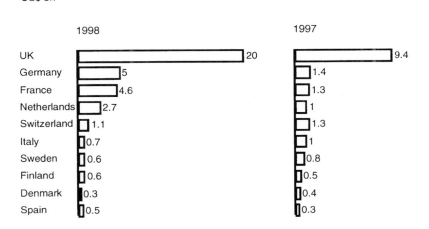

Sources: Financial Times, Initiative Europe, KPMG

Figure 2.40   Value of buyouts by country, 1997–8

of deals, but some of the increase is a result of more valuable transactions taking place. In Germany, for example, the number of deals rose from 23 to 47 between 1996 and 1998. 1999 as a whole may turn out even better than earlier years. In 1999 most private equity funds, for example, have allocated 50 per cent of their European volume, a sum of US$30 bn, to Germany. Industry experts suggest that this money may not all be profitably employed, since in 1998, only US$8 bn had been targeted at Germany.[46]

Summary

Europe is amongst the most attractive regions in the world for many investment-banking businesses, with high growth rates, attractive fee levels and low capital requirements. On the continent especially, growth rates in M&A, equity issuance and debt origination have been healthy, aided by restructuring in the industrial sector, favourable market conditions and the launch of the common currency. Not all of this has directly lent a helping hand to continental financial centres. The common currency in particular has encouraged a move away from country-based research, and trading and sales teams in equities and fixed income. Instead, teams now cover all of the EMU area from one location – often London – organized along sectoral or maturity lines. At the same time, there has been an increase in the number of origination specialists being placed in Frankfurt and Paris. Also, some firms have begun to support them with complete execution teams. The success of these firms – such as Goldman Sachs in Germany – may cause more of their competitors to follow suit.

TRADE IN FINANCIAL SERVICES

Export performance is a standard measure of competitiveness. Being able to sell abroad often implies either a cheaper or a higher-quality product, or the satisfaction of consumers' preference for diversity. Here the trading pattern of European countries is used to evaluate their comparative performance. Primarily, this reflects their standing in the most globalized products. It is important to bear in mind that it says little about the quality or quantity of financial services provided domestically, which may well be more important in terms of value added and the externalities generated.

Documenting the overall magnitude and growth of this area of world trade, it is important to note here that it is only recently that the IMF balance of payment manual for reporting international transactions has started to show a clear distinction between services and income.[47] Trade in services represents only a small part of the global total. In 1997, for every $1 of

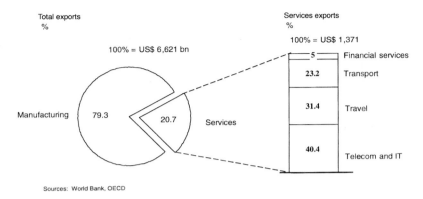

Sources: World Bank, OECD

Figure 2.41 Composition of trade, 1997

service exports, there were almost $4 in manufactured exports. In turn, trade
in financial services only represents a small share of the trade in services,
at some 5 per cent (Figure 2.41). However, no other good or service has
witnessed similar rates of growth in the period 1980–97. The value of
financial services exports has increased almost fivefold; over the same
period, growth in trading manufactured goods has only tripled.
Interestingly, financial services are ahead even compared with major areas
of growth in international trade, such as telecommunications/information
technology (IT) and travel.[48]

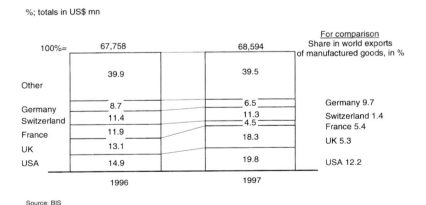

Source: BIS

Figure 2.42 Market share of selected countries in world financial services exports,
1996–7

Despite overall growth, not all countries have achieved higher volumes. In terms of total exports of financial services by value, the US and the UK lead the world. Switzerland generates the third-highest export volume in the world, despite its limited size. Germany and France follow, but at a respectable distance; German export levels are only slightly more than half of Swiss ones, or approximately one-third of the UK's. France trails with a mere US$3.1 bn in financial services exported in 1997 (Figure 2.42).[49]

A look at the pattern of imports reveals interesting contrasts. Only two of the countries examined in Figure 2.43 specialize in financial services across the board. Neither the UK nor Switzerland relies on imports to any significant extent; their export volumes do not reflect a skewed specialization in certain financial services, but signal a general competitive advantage in this small but rapidly growing segment of world trade.[50] The export balances of the US, Germany and France are significantly reduced because of sizeable financial service imports. This suggests that their financial sectors do not have a comparative advantage across the full range of financial services, but rely crucially on imports from other countries to satisfy home demand. While the US and Germany's levels of import penetration are relatively similar (amounting to approximately three-quarters of total exports), France has an almost completely balanced position in trading financial services. Its imports are sufficiently large to reduce the overall balance to 10 per cent of export volume.

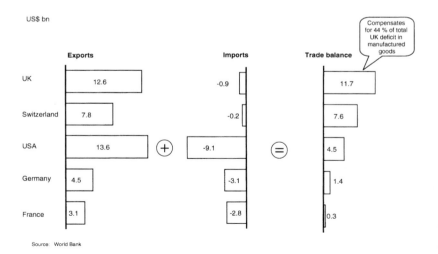

Figure 2.43   Exports and imports of financial services,[51] 1997

In 1997 there was a rapid rise in the concentration of financial services exports.[52] The combined share of the US, the UK and Switzerland jumped by 10 percentage points. The top three countries thus had 49 per cent of world trade in financial services, compared with 39 per cent one year earlier. Together, these three countries accounted for close to one-half of total world exports in financial services. Conversely, trends over time point to a remarkable decline in the competitiveness of the French financial services sector. The World Bank figures not only suggest a decline in market share, but an absolute fall in export values. The change in position does not appear to be the result of erratic year-by-year movement, since French financial service exports were equivalent to 14 per cent of the world total in 1995. This suggests that the sharp decline shown in Figure 2.42 is part of a long-term trend. German market share also fell to 6.5 per cent from 8.7 per cent – a change not as dramatic as in the French case, but also rapid. Nearly all the gains accrued to the UK and the US. The UK gained more than 5 percentage points, and the US took an additional 4.9 per cent of the world market. The increase in concentration therefore largely reflects changes in the position within the top five financial services exporters. The total market share of the top five barely changed at all.

Disaggregated statistics for the UK allow a closer look at the source of export earnings. The US and Switzerland are the two largest customers of UK financial service exports; Germany comes third, contributing some 14 per cent to total UK revenues. Of the total, securities dealers are the largest single source of export earnings, bringing in 42 per cent. Monetary financial institutions come second, taking a little over half the total.

To illustrate the importance of trade in financial services for the UK economy, its direct impact on employment can be approximated by comparing export balances with value added per employee. The UK's trade surplus in 1996 was equivalent to the value added of 112,000 employees; relative to the number of employees in the City of London (approximately 155,000 in 1996), this is not a small figure. Germany, in contrast, has a much lower market share. If its performance in financial services were on par with its exports market share in manufactured goods, it could gain value added equivalent to 17,000 employees.[53] Note also that these significant employment effects exist despite the unusually high value added per employee in financial services, which does reduce the estimated impact.

Trade is not a zero-sum game. Specialization and the exploitation of comparative advantage boost incomes all round. This applies to financial services no less than it does to trade in manufactured goods. Germany remains the world's second-largest goods exporter, despite a high cost base and adverse exchange-rate fluctuations. But Germany's national income may not be maximized if the development of a financial services sector involves an inefficient allocation of resources. In striking contrast, the UK has made up for its weakness in manufacturing (with a decline in export share from 6.6 to 5.3 per cent) by its growing strength in invisibles. Of course, classic trade theory in the spirit of Heckscher and Ohlin explained patterns of trade through differences in factor endowments. Analysis that is ultimately based on the gifts of nature is less compelling when it comes to analysing trade in financial services – where the ultimate resource is skilled personnel – that largely takes place between highly developed countries.[54] This overview of performance gleaned from trade figures indicates the strengthening position of the UK and the squeezing out of France and, to a lesser extent, of Germany. However, this may not be true for all financial services and also may not reflect the position in the product areas focused on the domestic rather than the international market.

These developments are much more in line with what, since the 1970s, has become known as the 'New Trade Theory'. It emphasizes increasing returns as an important cause of trade, and offers a ready explanation why most of world trade today occurs between countries at very similar levels of development.[55]

THE COST OF REGULATION

Regulations cause costs at three levels. First, there is the direct cost of regulators' pay and the enforcement process. Second, compliance with national rules and regulations can also impose costs on firms, which can be very considerable, but are hard to estimate. Third, there are the very real disadvantages suffered by firms if they are unable to conduct certain kinds of transactions or are kept from making certain improvements to their processes due to regulatory barriers. There is one short cut that has so far been used to estimate the cost of regulation. This is to allocate personnel and other costs at national regulators to the individual elements of the securities industry, and then assume certain multiples for compliance costs.

Direct costs vary strongly by industry subgroup. Securities trading is the area that attracts the highest regulatory costs due to the complexity and frequency of transactions involved. The UK has the lowest regulatory costs in securities trading out of the three countries for which we currently have available data. France has regulatory costs almost four times as high as the UK, with the US in a middle position. Investment management can also be heavily regulated, and causes considerable costs in the UK. In the US and France, the cost is much lower. In the case of life assurance,

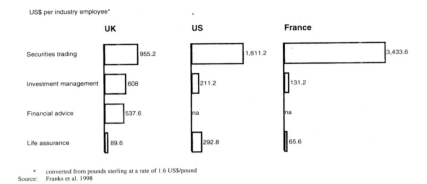

* converted from pounds sterling at a rate of 1.6 US$/pound
Source:　Franks et al. 1998

Figure 2.44　Direct regulatory costs

however, the US has the highest cost base. Unfortunately, there is no data available for Germany.

The UK advantage in securities trading is not a result of lower salaries – on the contrary. On average, for each regulator, the UK paid (including all other expenses) £131,000, compared with £102,000 in France and £101,000 in the US. The main reason for low regulatory costs is the use of a small number of regulators relative to the size of the sector. While there are 6.5 times more people employed in securities trading in the UK than in France, the number of regulators is not even twice as high. Nor are economies of scale the true reason for lower costs. The US has 3.5 times as many people employed in trading as the UK, but uses 12 times more staff. Measured against operating expenses, a similar story emerges. While the UK imposes direct regulatory costs of 0.52 per cent of operating expenses, the corresponding figure for the US is 1.09 per cent (figures for France are not available). In investment management, the UK adds 17 bp in regulatory costs relative to the funds under management. Here, France appears to be the most efficient, with just 4 bp, and the US is in second place with 9 bp.

This, of course, does not fully account for the cost of regulation. Compliance costs are very substantial, adding to legal expenses, systems expenditure, training costs and custody, as well as the hiring of in-house compliance staff. There are, however, no good estimates on an international basis. The UK is the only country for which we have full survey-based data. There, for every £1 of direct costs, there are about £4 in indirect costs. Firms estimate that 37 per cent of this sum would be incurred even if there was no regulatory pressure.[56]

The final category of regulatory costs is hardest to assess quantitatively. National rules and regulations may prevent improvements and rationalizations, and sometimes make certain kinds of transactions altogether impossible. Most of the obvious difficulties on the continent (such as the prohibition of derivatives trading, and so on) have been reduced or overcome in recent years. Nonetheless, rules and regulations that are not specific to the financial services sector sometimes continue to impinge significantly on the conduct of business. The possibility of cross-border data processing in Germany is the most egregious example – global investment banks that want to pool their data processing in one location run foul of the problem that, according to current practice, data used by the German investment bank has to be hosted on a German server, and not be made available automatically in locations abroad. In effect, the only location where world-wide records and data can be kept is in Germany itself; insofar as this does not happen to be the most sensible solution, the bank will only be able to chose between the inefficiency of the wrong location and the inefficiency of not pooling data-processing equipment and personnel at all. Whenever personal data is involved, the barriers to organizational excellence become even more onerous.

THE EYE OF THE BEHOLDER: BUSINESSMEN'S PERCEPTIONS

To a certain extent, the beauty of financial markets is in the eye of the beholder. When it comes to being seen as capital markets-friendly, the impressions of businessmen are relevant – even if they are based on misperceptions rather than reality. The World Economic Forum's Competitiveness Reports contain surveys of 2,000 businessmen from all over the world. Amongst other issues, they are also asked to comment on the sophistication of financial markets, the openness of bond and stock-markets, and the quality of regulation.[57]

Differences between countries are not large. In the list of 59 countries on which the World Economic Forum gathers views, all the countries analysed in this book consistently rank in the top 15 and no country ever scores less than 5.33 on a scale from 1 to 7. However, since the truly low scores apply to developing countries such as the Ukraine, even relatively small differences are relevant for our purposes.

The US is widely seen as the most stringent regulator of capital markets. At the same time, it has the most open bond and equity markets and the most sophisticated products. Within Europe, the UK is clearly the first, trailing the US by no more than a tiny margin in terms of sophistication and regulation. Switzerland comes third in three out of four categories. France

score on a scale from 1 (worst) to 7 (best)

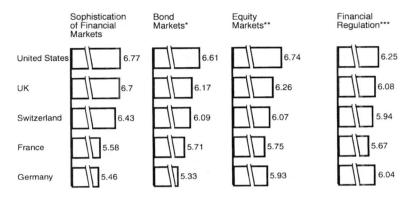

	Sophistication of Financial Markets	Bond Markets*	Equity Markets**	Financial Regulation***
United States	6.77	6.61	6.74	6.25
UK	6.7	6.17	6.26	6.08
Switzerland	6.43	6.09	6.07	5.94
France	5.58	5.71	5.75	5.67
Germany	5.46	5.33	5.93	6.04

*   Bond markets are highly developed for public and corporate finance
**   Stock markets are open to new firms and medium-sized firms
***   Regulation and supervision of financial institutions is among the world's most stringent
Source: World Economic Forum 1999

Figure 2.45   Competitiveness survey: financial markets, 1999

is a whisker ahead of Germany in terms of sophistication, and the quality and ease of access to bond and equity markets. In terms of regulation, however, it comes at the very bottom of our group. Germany is not seen as the most sophisticated market, and in terms of access to bonds and equity financing, it does not win plaudits from businessmen. In contrast, the quality of regulation is highly regarded, trailing behind the UK score by a mere 0.04.

SUMMARY: COMPETITIVE PROFILES

The picture that emerges from our analysis by product category is ambiguous. In some areas, such as forex trading and OTC derivatives, London's already impressive lead is growing rapidly. In others, continental competitors appear to be catching up fast. The competitive profiles of each financial centre are analysed by ranking product areas by the growth rates in each, and then examining: the market share that each financial centre can claim, calculated as the proportion of the business done by 'Europe's big three' capital cities;[58] and the change in position in the recent past.[59]

Germany's gains in market share are greatest in the product areas with relatively slow growth. These are the products in which Germany also has a high market share already: cross-border lending, exchange-traded derivatives and equity issuance. In the areas of highest growth, however, market share is often around 15 per cent of total 'big three' business, with few signs of growth. Clearly, growth rates alone are not all that can be said about market attractiveness. However, it can serve a first approximation for our purposes.

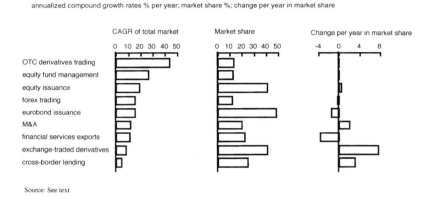

annualized compound growth rates % per year; market share %; change per year in market share

Figure 2.46   Competitive profile: Germany

France shows a similar pattern, but has fewer clear strengths. In the group of high-growth products, it is losing market share in equity fund management, while showing slow gains in OTC derivatives and forex trading. In exchange-traded derivatives, cross-border lending and financial service exports, its performance is weak and deteriorating rapidly.

Where France manages to show growth, it is in the size of domestic markets rather than the share of value generated nationally.

The UK has more than 50 per cent market share in six out of nine categories. It also has first position in seven out of nine categories. In some high-growth areas, it is gaining market share – modestly in OTC derivatives and forex trading, markedly in equity fund management and Eurobond issuance. It export performance continues to be very strong, showing gains in market share over time. But in M&A, equity issuance and exchange-traded derivatives, it is losing market share.

What, then, of the overall scorecard? London enjoys a commanding lead in many fast-growing areas, but some of these are arguably amongst the least attractive businesses. In forex trading, for example, margins are wafer-

Source: see text

*Figure 2.*47   Competitive profile: France

annualized compound growth rates % per year; market share %; change per year in market share

Source: See text

*Figure 2.*48   Competitive profile: UK

thin and declining, requiring the use of large amounts of capital to capture significant profits. In those areas, however, where the size of the domestic market matters, it is no longer no contest between the UK and the continentals. Germany (and, to a lesser extent, France) are showing rapid gains in the businesses that matter most when it comes to harnessing the power of capital markets for economic growth, such as equity issuance and M&A. At the same time, these are precisely the product areas where value added is largest, and where domestic provision of services improves their quality significantly.

3 Financial Centres, Capital Market Performance and the Economy

This chapter considers the benefits to the economy that could arise from encouraging the use of a wider range of financial services. Financial services contribute both directly and indirectly to economic growth, via the value added in the sector itself, and through the indirect benefits the sector provides for the rest of the economy through more efficient investment, risk allocation, corporate governance and aggregation of savings. First, the most immediate contribution of financial centres, the employment and value added they create, is examined, followed by a consideration of the less direct – and potentially more important – benefits.

BRINGING HOME THE BACON

Value added in financial services per employee is at least twice the level observed in the rest of the economy. In the US in 1996, the level stood at three times the economy average. Significantly, the lead was particularly strong in the case of securities dealers (Figure 3.1). In these wholesale businesses (as opposed to retail businesses, which involve direct contact with private end-users), value added per head in the US in 1996 was US$203,416 (equivalent to 3.3 times the economy-wide average). The UK showed a similar picture, with financial services generating value added almost 75 per cent higher than the rest of the economy.

Over time, the financial services industry's output per employee has been highly volatile. Good years in the late 1980s and in 1992/3 (and again, over the last three years 1995–8) have alternated with some bad years, especially 1994. Figure 3.2 gives average value added per employee in investment banks for 1988–97. Since these have often merged with brokerage houses, two groups are used: one of all the firms (unadjusted), and the second of only those that were in observation for the full sample period while pursuing nothing but investment-banking activities.[60]

Labour productivity growth in the sector has been uneven; in the UK, value added per employee has surged by 17.8 per cent since 1992, while in the US the increase was a mere 7 per cent. Significantly, securities dealers

1996 US$

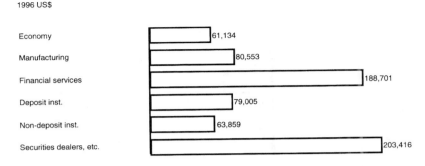

Source: ONS

Figure 3.1   Value added per head, US, 1996

(in the US, where disaggregated statistics are available) saw the value of their total output over the period rise by 31.7 per cent, putting them ahead even of manufacturing industry in the US. Total factor productivity in the US also increased considerably, most notably in securities dealing (rising by 41.2 per cent). In the UK, financial services as a whole showed the highest rate of total factor productivity increase with 14.3 per cent, ahead of manufacturing (Figure 3.3).

The total size of the financial services sector in general, and of investment banking in particular, is fairly limited. Although financial services (broadly defined to include financial services, insurance and

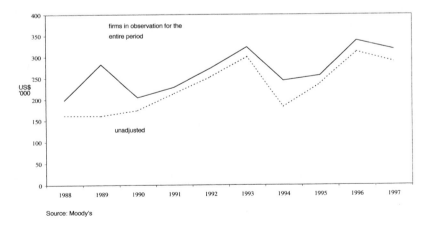

Source: Moody's

Figure 3.2   Value added per employee in investment banks, 1988–97

%

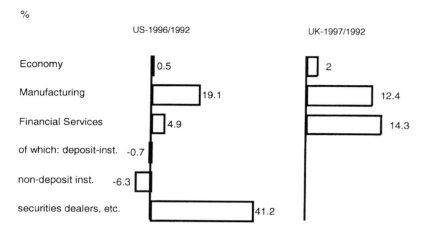

Source: ONS

Figure 3.3   Growth of value added relative to total factor input, UK and US

property/real estate) are important and growing sectors of the economy, contributing some 25 per cent and 18 per cent of GDP in the UK and US respectively in 1996, the contribution of investment banking on its own is less impressive. Employment too is not extensive. In the UK just over 4 per cent of its workforce are employed in financial intermediation. In the US nearly 6 per cent are thus employed, but only 8.5 per cent of these are involved in security and broking activities. Even in the countries that lead the world in financial services, the sector is small.

LIQUIDITY MEASURES AND THE COMPOSITION OF EXTERNAL FINANCING

In addition to some job creation, the financial sector facilitates the efficient working of other sectors of the economy by matching financing needs with supply through the provision of instruments and information on investment possibilities. An efficient financial system can thereby help to mobilize investment within the economy. One of the most important functions provided by financial systems is liquidity, the ability to convert assets into ready cash. Financing based on securities offers one important advantage to the investor over other forms of financing, which is a higher degree of liquidity. The actual degree of liquidity attained depends on the ease with which claims can be traded, and the extent to which financial instruments are actually tradable in capital markets.

On both measures, European countries continue to differ significantly. The mix of total external financing shows the extent to which countries have embraced solutions based on capital markets. Financial systems oriented towards capital markets use (domestic) bank credit and equity financing in about equal measure. Bank-dominated systems like Germany and France use many times more bank credit than market-based financing. This causes their respective national totals to lag considerably behind their European rivals, the UK and Switzerland (Figure 3.4).

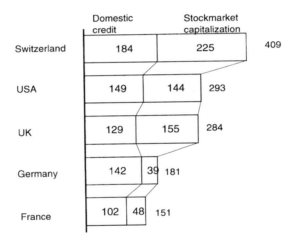

% of GDP

	Domestic credit	Stockmarket capitalization	
Switzerland	184	225	409
USA	149	144	293
UK	129	155	284
Germany	142	39	181
France	102	48	151

Sources: World Bank, IMF

Figure 3.4   Value of total external financing, 1997

Changes over time have not been uniform. Most countries' market capitalization relative to GDP increased rapidly between 1990 and 1997, but trends in domestic credit provided by the banking sector diverged. Germany, for example, started with bank credit equivalent to 110 per cent of GDP in 1990, and had added 31.5 per cent to this figure by 1997. Over the same period, domestic bank lending in France declined marginally from 106.3 per cent of GDP to 102.2 per cent. The UK also maintained an almost constant ratio of bank-financed debt to GDP, whereas there was an increase in the US from 114.4 per cent to 148.7 per cent.[61] Market capitalization relative to GDP almost tripled in the US over the same period. It more than tripled in Switzerland, and almost doubled in France, the UK and Germany. Current differences are therefore the result of superior asset returns and faster growth in stockmarket listings in the US and Switzerland, as well as continued growth in bank lending in Germany.

In terms of stockmarket liquidity itself, Germany enjoyed a significant lead over its European rivals in 1996–7 (Figure 3.5). No other country's stockmarket came close to turning shares over with similar frequency. In 1997, German aggregate market liquidity was twice French levels, and three times the UK's.[62] In 1997, the gap between the German market and its rivals widened still further. While in 1996 Germany was 18 percentage points ahead of its nearest European rival, Switzerland, this differential had widened to 39 percentage points one year later.

These figures suggest that the limited macroeconomic role of the German stockmarket is solely the result of limited market capitalization. The most liquid stockmarket in Europe, in combination with its limited size relative to GDP, results in a paltry turnover ratio (the value of all shares traded

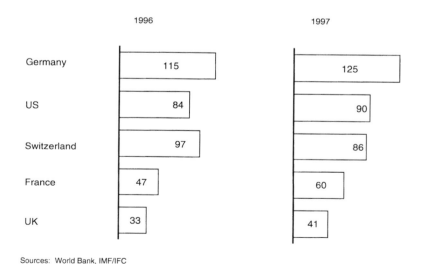

Sources: World Bank, IMF/IFC

Figure 3.5   Stockmarket liquidity, 1996–7

relative to GDP). Figure 3.6 shows the two factors that determine this statistic. Switzerland dominates all European rivals, and is even ahead of the US on this count. The UK shows a higher figure than Germany, which in turn is substantially ahead of France. German market size is primarily limited by the low numbers of firms listing on the stock exchange. Despite a lower total GDP, the UK market had 2,046 domestic listings in 1997, compared with 700 in Germany.

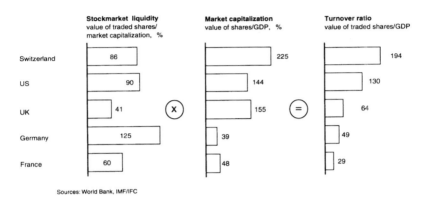

Figure 3.6   Determinants of turnover ratios, 1996–7

RETURNS FOR INVESTORS

Asset returns have proved spectacular in most Western countries over the years 1995–9. In the longer term (since the 1920s), however, the US and Switzerland have been the only countries in the world showing substantial excess returns of 4.5 per cent and 3.3 per cent per year respectively. Nominal returns have been good in France, the US and the UK, but persistent inflation has eroded many of these gains. Compared with the long-term average of real returns, recent performance in all markets appears unusually high, with annual real returns in most countries of above 10 per cent per year. Political stability appears to be a prerequisite for substantial excess returns.[63]

In the 1990s, stockmarket performance across Europe has varied substantially (Figure 3.8). Figures for the US are given for comparison. Average nominal returns have been most spectacular in Switzerland and the UK, but accounting for risk, neither one of them has matched US performance. German equity returns marginally outpaced British ones (12 per cent per year as against 11.3 per cent per year), but only at the expense

% per year

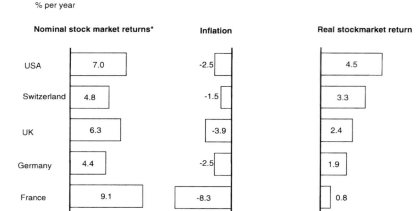

Nominal stock market returns*   **Inflation**   **Real stockmarket return**

USA	7.0	-2.5	4.5
Switzerland	4.8	-1.5	3.3
UK	6.3	-3.9	2.4
Germany	4.4	-2.5	1.9
France	9.1	-8.3	0.8

* annually compounded
Source: Jorion and Goetzmann 1999

Figure 3.7   Stockmarket performance and inflation in selected countries, January 1921–December 1996

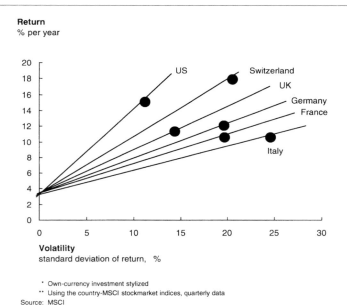

Return
% per year

* Own-currency investment stylized
** Using the country-MSCI stockmarket indices, quarterly data
Source: MSCI

Figure 3.8   Risk and return in selected asset markets*, 1990–8

of considerably higher volatility. Whereas UK domestic investors had to accept volatility on a scale of 14.4 per cent annually, the figure for Germany was 19.6 per cent. French investors in their local market experienced volatility on the same scale as Germans, but received a lower return overall. Of all the European markets, Italy fared worst, with both the lowest return and the highest volatility of all markets considered.

The average for the 1990s may not be doing justice to markets that have recently seen significant changes in their regulatory environment, organization and the investment attitudes of the wider public. Examining the period 1995–8 shows some interesting changes in relative positions (Figure 3.9). The US continues to dominate any investment choice open domestically to European investors, and Switzerland retains its dominant position on the continent. At the bottom end of the league table, Italy and France have retained their relative positions, with Italy continuing to offer the lowest returns combined with the highest volatility. The German market has gained ground. It now offers a combination of risk and return on par with the UK market; German domestic investors face both lower risk and higher returns than French ones.

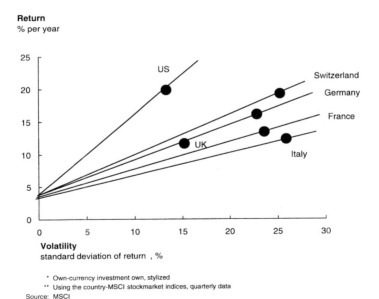

Figure 3.9   Risk and return in selected asset markets,* 1995–8

Opportunities available to investors have increased in recent years with the listing of young and medium-sized firms on specially created markets, often with a focus on high-tech. The most successful addition to the German equity market, in 1997, has been the Neuer Markt, aimed at young, high-growth firms. By any standard, the Neuer Markt has turned in a spectacular performance. Over the years 1997–8, volatility was only marginally higher than in the German stockmarket at large, yet returns were an annualized 87 per cent. The US equivalent to the Neuer Markt, NASDAQ, offered significantly lower returns. Despite lower volatility as well, the overall risk-return profile was less favourable. New markets in Benelux countries also offered attractive returns without extreme volatility. At the bottom of the performance table was until recently the Nouveau Marché, the French equivalent to Germany's Neuer Markt (Figure 3.10).

Another way to assess these markets for rapidly growing technology firms is to compare their performances after opening. In the 27 months after the first index figures were compiled for NASDAQ, the Nouveau Marché and the Neuer Markt, neither the US nor the French market came close to matching the price performance of Frankfurt's Neuer Markt, whose technology stocks were up 500 per cent, whilst the other markets struggled

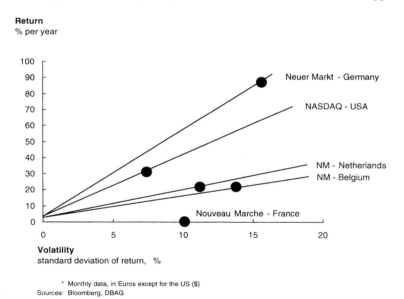

Figure 3.10   Risk and return in selected stockmarkets for young, fast-growing companies

to yield a positive return at all. The Nouveau Marché languished in negative territory since its inception, and NASDAQ investors were not even beginning to realize any of the superior returns that were to come later in the 1980s and 1990s.

CHANGES IN FINANCIAL WEALTH

Individuals, or households, can grow richer in two ways: by saving more, or by investing in assets yielding a (real) return. Savings rates and investment choices differ markedly in various countries. Total wealth relative to household income differs by about 20 per cent from top to bottom between the US, UK, Germany and France. Differences in the composition of this wealth are much more dramatic. While US and UK savers held more than half of their assets in financial wealth, French investors were slightly more in favour of 'real' wealth (largely real estate), and Germans kept less than one-third of their wealth in financial assets (Figure 3.11).

In 1997, the average US household had net financial assets equivalent to 378 per cent of net disposable household income; the UK figure was 337 per cent.[64] France ranked third, with 210 per cent, followed by Germany, which recorded 144 per cent (Figure 3.12).[65] Figure 3.12 shows changes in net financial wealth for 1992–7. The UK and France increased the value of financial assets per head by some 50 per cent; the US and Germany trailed behind by more than 10 percentage points. Interestingly, changes in wealth show little correlation with household savings rates. Germany, with the second-highest savings rate, comes bottom of the table, while the UK and

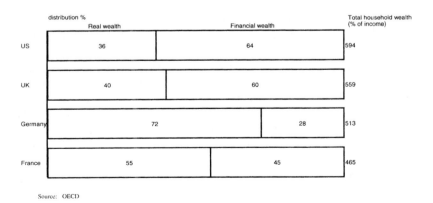

Figure 3.11   Net real and financial wealth, 1997

1992=100

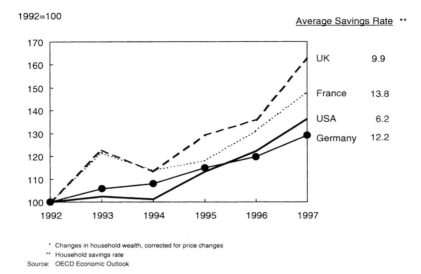

Average Savings Rate **

UK	9.9
France	13.8
USA	6.2
Germany	12.2

```
170
160
150
140
130
120
110
100
    1992   1993   1994   1995   1996   1997
```

* Changes in household wealth, corrected for price changes
** Household savings rate
Source: OECD Economic Outlook

Figure 3.12   Changes in net financial wealth per household,* 1992–7

US, with single-digit savings rates, record rapid increases in financial wealth per head.

The reasons for this apparent paradox become obvious when rates of return between 1983 and 1997 are considered. These can only be inferred indirectly for all assets, not just financial ones, so that the figures are partly driven by the mix of real and financial assets. The US records average (implied) real rates of return of 3 per cent, with the UK following with 1.8 per cent.[66] France and Germany trail by a considerable margin, recording average levels of return of 0.4 per cent and 0.3 per cent respectively.[67] Nor were the high returns in Anglo-Saxon countries bought at the price of higher risk, since the coefficient of variation of asset returns was lowest for the US, followed by the UK. French investors faced considerable risks, with a coefficient of variation nine times the US level.[68] US investors only experienced negative returns in two years, and the UK and France saw negative returns in five out of twelve years. Germans fared even worse: only in every second year did they earn positive (real) returns. The picture changes little if we focus on the period since 1993, where data comparability is better. Again, the US comes out on top, with an average annual real return of 4 per cent, followed by the UK with 0.8 per cent. France achieves 0.4 per cent, and Germany 0.6 per cent.

Table 3.1   Real asset returns for US, UK, France and Germany

	US	UK	France	Germany
1985–6	8.1%	24.1%	5.6%	
1986–7	1.3%	–9.0%	–5.4%	
1987–8	3.5%	14.2%	4.2%	
1988–9	3.4%	4.9%	2.9%	
1989–90	–3.8%	–8.7%	–6.3%	
1990–1	2.2%	–3.9%	3.7%	(–16.1%*)
1991–2	0.5%	–5.0%	–1.8%	–1.2%
1992–3	0.7%	7.0%	3.6%	0.3%
1993–4	–0.7%	–8.0%	–6.2%	–0.5%
1994–5	7.2%	3.2%	–0.9%	1.6%
1995–6	5.5%	0.9%	2.4%	–0.1%
1996–7	7.9%	NA	3.1%	1.7%
Mean	3%	1.8%	0.4%	0.3%
Mean 1993–8	4.0%	0.8%	0.4%	0.6%
standard deviation	3.7%	10.5%	4.3%	1.2%
Number of years with negative returns	2/12	5/12	5/12	3/6

Note: * Returns disregarded due to break in series because of reunification.

Disappointing realized rates of return, as well as lower household wealth relative to income, suggest that continental savers are leaving big bills sitting on the sidewalk. Why should this be? Total leverage does not appear to be a contributing factor. The ratio of financial assets to net financial assets stands at a high of 1.55 in Germany compared with 1.33 in France and the UK, with the US recording a lower level of 1.27. Given that the country with the lowest rate of return is the most highly leveraged, while the others show rather little borrowing, there appears little reason to believe that leverage is a good way of accelerating asset growth.[69] The level of equity holdings relative to household income provides more conclusive evidence. This ranges from 18 per cent in Germany to 133 per cent in the US in 1997.

Most households in the countries under discussion appear to hold very considerable amounts of cash, thereby depressing returns. Of the total flow of savings between 1984 and 1996, 42 per cent were acquiring cash (or similar assets, such as cash and deposits) in France, compared with 44 per cent in Germany and 57 per cent in the US. The UK, in contrast, records a mere 37 per cent going into cash and similar instruments. The difficulty of earning a positive real return (after tax) on bonds and savings accounts is partly responsible for the results in Table 3.1.[70]

Over the past decade, the Germans and the French have been active buyers of corporate equity securities, investing 9 per cent (Germany) and 15 per cent (France) of new savings in shares. The UK actually records a reduction in holdings of corporate equities of 10 per cent; as many firms are buying back their shares, private holdings are necessarily reduced. In the US, there have been little new direct purchases of equities. Note, however, that these figures do not take account of saving in equity mutual funds, so that households may be increasing their equity exposure without being recorded under this particular heading.

The sophistication of investment decisions is also influenced by the extent to which households retain the services of institutional investors. Largely because of differences in pension systems, the percentage of household assets managed by institutional investors varies considerably. In 1996, while France came bottom with 27 per cent, Germany recorded 29 per cent. The UK showed the highest proportion, with more than half (52 per cent) of all assets managed by institutional investors. The US came second, with 45 per cent of assets.

The above considerations can be aggregated into a financial literacy index. A maximum of 4 points are awarded. The second-ranked receives 3, and so on, and the last country receives only 1 point. Five categories are used: the percentage of assets managed by institutions, the percentage of equity holdings relative to household income, the percentage of wealth held in financial assets, the leverage ratio and the savings rate. The last two are not measures of literacy; rather, they represent costs to the household, either real or potential. Higher savings rates imply a greater share of income sacrificed for wealth acquisition; higher leverage ratios imply greater risks.[71] But higher-equity holdings, a greater proportion of assets managed by institutions, or a reduced preference for so-called 'real' wealth all tend to be signs of greater financial sophistication amongst the investing public. Countries that save much will therefore receive a low score. If they then hand over little of their assets to institutional investors – that is, they receive a high score in terms of the ranking – then their overall financial literacy is recorded as low. To achieve asset growth, they rely on abstention, not delegation of asset management. In the reverse case, with low leverage rates (lower risks) and high equity holdings, the overall score shows greater sophistication. In all likelihood, wealth will grow because of superior asset returns, not because of greater leverage. Table 3.2 gives an overview of the results.

The US records the highest score for financial literacy, with the lowest leverage ratio and the lowest savings rate, combined with high levels of equity and financial wealth holdings. It also achieved high rates of return

financial literacy, real rate of return % per year

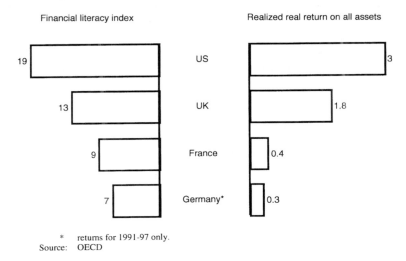

* returns for 1991-97 only.
Source: OECD

Figure 3.13   Financial literacy and realized rate of return, 1985–97

for the years 1985–97 (Figure 3.13). Germany trails behind: Germans are keen to make financial provision, as evidenced by a high savings rate, but a small proportion of total wealth held in the form of financial assets, combined with low equity holdings and a limited role for institutions, led to lower returns, considerable volatility – and the lowest score. The UK's equity holdings and emphasis on institutional investors are similar to those of the US, and returns overall even exceed those realized in the US. France's scores are more similar to its continental neighbour, coming out third in the index because of the high savings rates, little involvement of institutions and moderate leverage.

Institutions are an important determinant of these savings and investment patterns. High savings rates on the continent may partly reflect some lack of trust in public pay-as-you-go pension schemes. High rates of equity ownership and institutional involvement in the UK and the US are partly driven by tax relief on defined-contribution retirement plans which are often administered by the large asset management firms, such as 401(k) and IRA accounts in America and PEPs or ISAs in the UK. The introduction of AS-mutual funds (targeted at retirement saving) in Germany may in time make a dent, but is unlikely to have a major impact until tax relief is provided.

Table 3.2　Financial literacy index: US, UK, France and Germany, 1997

		US	UK	France	Germany
Percentage	Percentage of assets held				
	by institutions	45.0%	52.0%	27.0%	29.0%
	Equity holdings[72]	61.5%	48.9%[73]	43.5%	4.9%[74]
	Financial wealth/total wealth	63.6%	60.1%	45.2%	28.0%
	Leverage ratio[75]	27.1%	33.3%	33.3%	53.1%
	Savings rate	2.2%	11.0%	14.6%	11.0%
Scores	Percentage of assets held				
	by institutions (1)	3	4	1	2
	Equity holdings (2)	4	2	3	1
	Financial wealth/total wealth (3)	4	3	2	1
	Leverage (4)	4	2	2	1
	Savings rate (5)	4	2	1	2
Financial literacy (sum 1–5)		19	13	9	7

INTERNATIONAL CAPITAL MARKET INTEGRATION

Investors' integration into the world capital market lowers the cost of capital for companies and improves the risk/return profile of investors' opportunity sets. This integration can be measured in terms of outcomes and input measures. There are three main measures of international capital market integration.

- size of portfolio flows relative to GDP
- equity market returns correlations
- real interest-rate convergence.

The first is a classic input measure; the others are output measures.

The size of international capital flows relative to GDP (portfolio investment only, therefore excluding direct investment) has increased in recent years, but swings from one year to the next have been considerable. In 1990–7 by far the largest participant in the international capital market on this measure was the UK, with annual flows of up to 18 per cent of GDP. By historical standards, these are high values (the last time similar figures were noted was for Argentina in the period 1870–89).[76] In Germany and France capital flows' importance grew, while the US, a large player in absolute terms, showed only modest levels of international capital market participation relative to its large GDP (Figure 3.14).

Capital outflows in 1997 were larger than capital inflows for all major countries in our sample except the US. The US and Switzerland came top

in percent

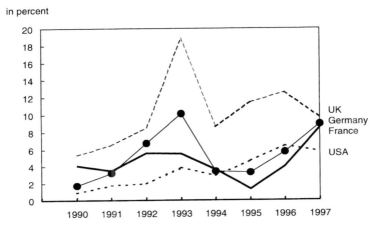

* Absolute value of change in assets plus absolute value of change in liabilities relative to GDP

Source: IMF

Figure 3.14   Capital flows relative to GDP,* 1990–7

in terms of non-residents' investment relative to GDP, and France finished last. Outflows were largest for Switzerland and the UK (Figure 3.15). The overall net balance in the US, necessary to fund the widening trade deficit, was largely a result of Americans investing little abroad, not of foreigners buying US assets on an unusual scale. The composition of flows also varied considerably between countries. France had not only one of the lowest shares of residents' investment abroad; it also registered the lowest proportion of equity investment in our sample. The US showed by far the highest proportion, with Germany, the UK and Switzerland occupying the middle ranks.

Given that figures change markedly from year to year, stocks of international investment may provide a more reliable guide than annual flows. In 1997, the UK records by far the highest level of total foreign holdings, equivalent to 137 per cent of GDP. The US and France follow at a respectable distance with 54 and 46 per cent, and Germany comes last. Interestingly, these low percentages are largely the result of continental citizens' investing less abroad. While the US, France and Germany show only approximately one-fifth of the UK's level of investment abroad relative to GDP, the non-residents' investments are closer to one-half the UK level.

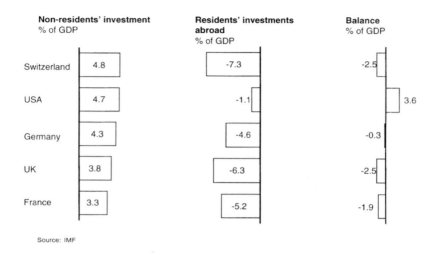

Figure 3.15   Flows of investment, 1997

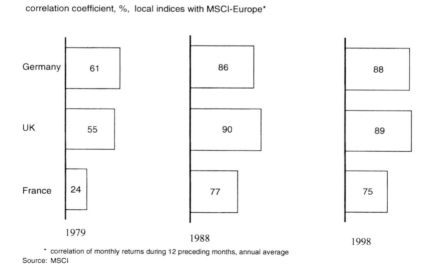

Figure 3.16   Market integration in Europe, 1979, 1988 and 1998

Taking a long-term perspective, market integration within Europe has increased a great deal. During the 1970s, the correlations between countries were modest – only Germany recorded a correlation above 0.6. Returns on the French stockmarket appeared almost entirely unrelated to movements elsewhere in Europe, with a correlation of 0.24. Between the 1970s and 1980s, market integration grew for all the major countries in our sample, with the UK showing the highest degree of market integration. Surprisingly, the 1990s have seen almost no changes. This is partly because return correlations were already very high in the late 1980s; however, there is still room for improvement for France.

Figure 3.17 sheds further light on these results. We need to avoid one problem: countries with large stockmarkets also enter the pan-European index with a high weight, and are more likely to show high correlations. Figure 3.17 depicts the average return correlation, during the 12 preceding months, of each country with all other European countries in continuous observation since 1980.[77] For some periods, market integration appears to be high, only to collapse during some brief, well-defined periods. Average correlations increased between 1988 and 1998, but this may be more to do with the absence of idiosyncratic shocks than real convergence. Responses to wider shocks, such as the partial collapse of the ERM in 1992 and the interest-rate rise in the US in 1994, were fairly constant across countries, but appear a little more pronounced in the UK and Germany.

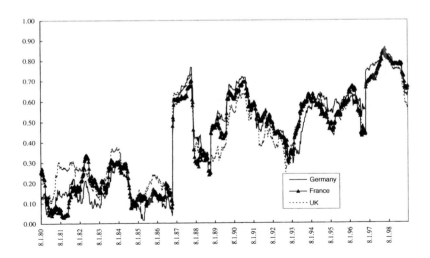

Figure 3.17   Correlation of equity markets, 1980–8

Our final measure of capital market integration is real interest-rate convergence, since with frictionless markets, real short-interest rates should be equal between countries. Figure 3.18 shows that this is true only to a limited extent in our sample. Since the beginning of the 1990s, overall dispersion has come down. Convergence between Germany and France has been particularly rapid in the run-up to the launch of the euro. The two countries which still show considerable divergence are Switzerland and the UK.

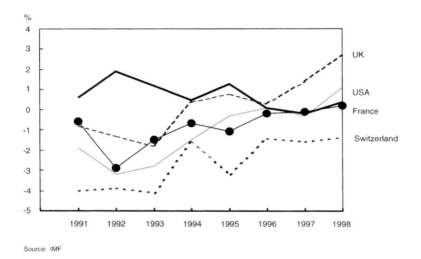

Source: IMF

Figure 3.18   Real interest rates: divergence from euro area mean, 1991–8

On the whole, capital market integration within Europe has increased. Firms should have benefited from lower costs of capital and wider sources of finance. Recent studies have argued that the cost of finance to firms may have declined by as much as 2 percentage points between 1992 and 1998.[78]

CORPORATE GOVERNANCE

Managers' aims and objectives often diverge from those of owners for a number of reasons – the so-called principal-agent problem. Overcoming these problems is one of the main functions of financial systems. Two approaches can be distinguished. Arm's-length systems grant considerable freedom of action to managers, and rely primarily on *ex post* reward or punishment of decision-makers by shareholders, with minimal meddling from other institutions. In contrast, command-and-control systems involve the close scrutiny of all major decisions by the stakeholders represented on the board. Instead of aligning incentives, outcomes are controlled.[79] Many writers have emphasized the extent to which oversight of companies by continental universal banks helps to reduce asymmetric information. By being represented on the board, banks can assess risks more adequately, as well as diminish them from the start – or so the story goes. In practice, these benefits have not always been readily apparent.[80] Disasters such as in the case of Metallgesellschaft or of Bremer Vulkan have left some observers wondering if effective oversight can really be exercised by boards of directors. At the same time, inquiries like the Cadbury Committee in the UK have highlighted the practical difficulties of operating a capital-markets based system.

To assess the quality of corporate governance in individual countries, a certain set of characteristics normally associated with good governance is measured. This is the approach taken by many surveys, such as the one in Figure 3.19, which shows the results for one of the most comprehensive ones, conducted by Heidrick and Struggles. It uses a set of seven characteristics normally associated with overcoming the principal-agent problem. The UK comes out on top (as might be expected from a ranking conducted by an Anglo-Saxon executive search firm). Of the countries examined more closely in this book, France beats Switzerland for second place; Germany lagging behind Switzerland is the result of a minuscule difference in the overall score. One important factor affecting Germany's score is the problem of disclosure, since neither in terms of background nor compensation is much information made available there. Germany scores particularly badly because of its failure to elect foreign directors. In the 40 firms surveyed, foreigners held an average of 31 per cent of all shares. On the board, however, they constituted a mere 5 per cent (compared with a European average of 18 per cent). France did markedly better, appointing some 14 per cent of board members from abroad, while 'insular' Britain even exceeded the European average. Its 19 per cent of directors from abroad puts it on par with Switzerland. It should be noted, however, that in Germany union representatives have to be elected to the board, making it much harder to raise the quota of foreigners. Peculiarities such as this also reveal the limits of the input-factor approach; cultural differences and individual preferences may have a major impact on the final ranking. The obvious way to avoid such problems is to measure results instead of inputs, the extent to which a corporate governance system is capable of delivering the goods.

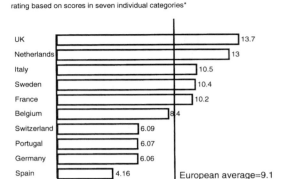

rating based on scores in seven individual categories*

*   Board structure (unitary or otherwise), proportion of non-executive directors, presence of foreign directors, disclosure of
     compensation, presence of board directors on board committees, use of specialized board committees, separate reporting of
     compliance with corporate governance criteria in the annual report
Source: Heidrick & Struggles (1999)

Figure 3.19   Corporate governance scores

The aim of corporate governance systems is to reward good management
and to punish poor performance. The final sanction is, of course, the
termination of the contract. How well do corporate governance systems
succeed in disciplining management? Our analysis is in the spirit of S.
Kaplan, who analysed the performance of US, Japanese and German
corporate governance systems.[81] Thus, the extent to which chief executive
officer (CEO) changes in the UK, Germany and France are associated with
a significant decline in operating performance, sales performance or share
price is analysed. The data used here cover the period 1990–7 and were
constructed as follows. The companies included are the 25 largest corporations in each of the three countries under consideration, as reported in the
1990 issue of *Fortune Magazine*'s top 500 international businesses. In order
to capture the role of banks in the three economies, ranking by sales or
assets was avoided. Instead, we focused on rankings by the number of
employees. Data availability difficulties reduced the number of companies
for which it was possible to gather relevant information to 24 for Germany
and France.

For every company in our sample, we used a set of four variables. Three
of them, market capitalization, sales and net income, are different measures
of performance, and the other two are intended to capture CEO turnover. A
dummy variable takes the value 1 if the CEO stays, and 0 otherwise.

Two data sources provide the relevant information. Moody's
International Manual provides information on the CEO, the composition of

the board of directors, net income, assets and sales. We obtained stock prices and the number of outstanding shares from Bloomberg. Figure 3.20 compares the percentage of cases when the CEO left in the same year as one of our performance measures records a decline, with the percentage when there was no decline. If there is effective monitoring and disciplining of bosses, we would expect the probability of leaving to be higher in those years when performance was unsatisfactory. Highlighted bars show the cases where there was a significant difference between CEO survival probability in good and bad years.

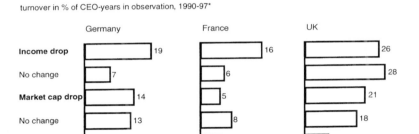

turnover in % of CEO-years in observation, 1990-97*

*   shaded bars indicate statistically significant divergence
Sources: Moody's, Bloomberg

Figure 3.20   CEO turnover and performance

All three countries appear to punish their top brass for underperformance to some extent. In Germany, a fall in the company's income increases a CEO's chances of being fired quickly, and a drop in sales also records a rise in CEO turnover by 6 percentage points.[82] Changes in market capitalization, however, are not a good predictor of CEO turnover. In France, there appears to be no penalty for a drop in sales (the figures actually suggest that the chances of being fired are actually higher if sales do not fall, but the difference is only marginally significant). In the case of income, however, the risk of being fired rises sharply if performance is below par.[83] UK managers need to worry little if income or sales fall. In the case of reductions in market capitalization, however, there is a real chance of losing one's job. Oddly, reductions in sales rarely coincide with the departure of the CEO.[84]

CAPITAL PRODUCTIVITY AND FINANCIAL CENTRE PERFORMANCE

Productivity is a crucial determinant of total output. It is driven by total output and the intensity of factor use. Only productivity underwrites the 'wealth of nations'; both higher rates of capital formation and intensive labour utilization have a direct negative impact on welfare.[85] Labour productivity has converged in most Organization for Economic Co-operation and Development (OECD) countries over the past 50 years as a result of catch-up, that is, the transfer of technology and organizational know-how from leading countries to followers.[86] Capital productivity, however, still varies considerably from one country to the next. Measurement is complicated by incompatibilities in the way national statistical bureaus compile capital stock estimates. Asset lives vary substantially, and it is difficult to ascertain how much of this variation accurately captures differences in actual asset durability, and how much is simply a result of arbitrary accounting conventions. However, work carried out by the McKinsey Global Institute (MGI) has dealt with most of these problems.[87] It has undertaken a major research project trying to standardize and compare accurately capital productivity estimates. In a number of studies, productivity levels were compared with the US.[88] These already contained all the required adjustments in levels, so we can derive first approximations of the comparative position of selected European countries in later years by using a combination of OECD output and capital stock estimates, and the original MGI results. In essence, we derive rates of change between the MGI study and 1998 from OECD data, and use these to adjust the figures calculated in the original McKinsey study.

Figure 3.21 shows the extent to which capital productivity differentials have persisted over the last few years. In 1990–3, Germany was a staggering 35 per cent behind US levels, and France was around 25 per cent less than US productivity. The UK was some 12 per cent behind. In 1998, the UK had all but closed the gap; it was arguably the only country in our sample approaching US capital productivity levels. Germany succeeded in narrowing the gap slightly, but the absolute difference remained large. France was, unusually, falling further behind the US and the UK.

The factors underlying the changes are detailed in Figure 3.22 for 1990–8. Output growth in France, Germany, the UK and the US were broadly similar, but changes in capital stock diverged. In Germany, the change of capital stock and total output was broadly equal, while the UK showed very slow expansion of its capital stock. Remarkably, the strong upsurge in US investment led to capital stock expansion outpacing output

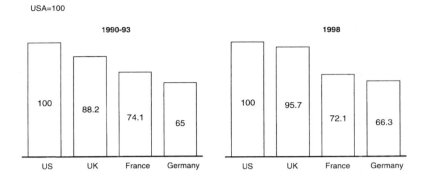

Figure 3.21   Capital productivity,* 1990–3 and 1998

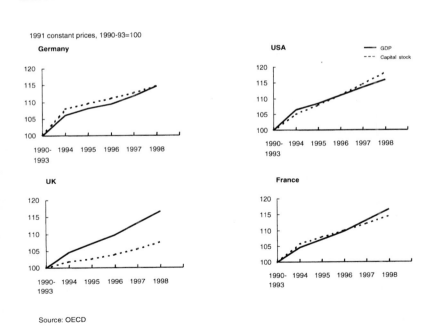

Figure 3.22   Change in output and capital stock, 1991 constant prices

growth; US capital productivity declined by 2 percentage points over the period, thus narrowing the gap with European countries.

German performance was actually somewhat better than Figure 3.21 suggests. Output per unit of capital equipment depends crucially on the efficiency of capital allocation as well as machine operating time. The flow of capital services, for any given stock of capital goods installed, is a product of both. Data on machinery operating times are not available on an annual basis, so instead we have used information on average hours worked per employee. This not only is usually available on an annual, and reliable, basis, but more importantly, this particular measure of labour input is highly correlated with machine running times.[89]

There has been a considerable divergence in house worked per employee between the US and Europe over the past 30 years. In 1970, the length of the annual working year was more or less the same in most OECD countries. Today, Americans work almost one-third more hours than their German counterparts. Since the beginning of the 1990s, the German gap has widened still further. In 1990–3, average hours per employee were 18 per cent below US levels, but this figure had increased to 21 per cent in 1998.[90] The figure for France was 14 per cent below US levels in 1990–3,

Hours per year, total employment

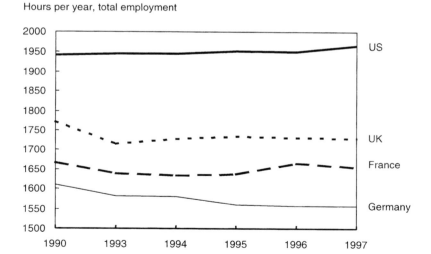

Source: OECD Economic Outlook

Figure 3.23   Labour input in selected economies, 1990–7

and widened only marginally to 15 per cent in 1997 (Figure 3.23). Absolute levels of labour input per year (and average machine operating hours) are still longer in France than in Germany, which explains most of the differential. These numbers imply that a growing proportion of the capital productivity gap is a result of union pressure for shorter hours as well as inflexible labour market arrangements; in contrast, the efficiency of capital allocation – despite the detrimental influence of tax policies – appears to have improved sufficiently to generate net gains.

The role of stockmarkets in improving capital allocation needs to be assessed carefully. Those countries having the most rapid increases in the value of share trading relative to GDP also improved capital productivity the fastest. The European laggard in this respect has been France, with a gain of merely 19 percentage points between 1990 and 1998. Here, the growing liquidity and relative importance of the stockmarket was apparently insufficient to neutralize the detrimental effects of shorter hours and government meddling in the allocation of capital. Especially in the case of high-growth companies, France has experienced little or no support from its capital markets – the Nouveau Marché has until recently disappointed investors and companies in equal measure. The UK's performance has been particularly good: working hours compared with the US declined by 2 per

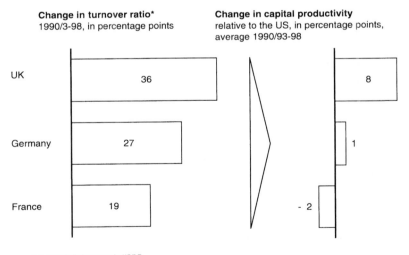

Change in turnover ratio*
1990/3-98, in percentage points

Change in capital productivity
relative to the US, in percentage points,
average 1990/93-98

UK	36	8
Germany	27	1
France	19	- 2

* Value of all shares traded/GDP
Sources: World Bank Development Indicators, OECD, McKinsey

Figure 3.24   Change in turnover ratio and capital productivity

cent, from a gap of 10 per cent to 12 per cent. Nonetheless, the capital productivity gap has shrunk dramatically. In 1990–3, UK capital productivity was almost 12 per cent behind the US; this gap was reduced in 1998 to less than 5 per cent. The staggering increase in stockmarket size and liquidity, as summarized by a rise in the turnover ratio of 36 percentage points between 1990 and 1998, coincided with this leap in capital productivity. This is eloquent testimony to the merits of unfettered capital markets and the crucial guidance that stockmarkets provide in the allocation of capital – the World Bank has found a strong correlation between the turnover ratio (as a summary measure of stockmarket liquidity and size), on the one hand, and output growth, on the other.[91]

Openness, measured as the proportion of exports and imports relative to GDP, is usually positively correlated with growth. Interestingly, recent evidence analysed by the World Trade Organization suggests that this is particularly true of trade in financial services. Most of the impact comes from increasing competition amongst intermediaries if tariffs for services are reduced. The growth impact of trade in financial services does not depend on export performance; being a large importer provides most of the benefits (as is generally the case with trade liberalization).[92]

SUMMARY

The benefits of having a competitive financial centre can be substantial. Direct effects are often sizeable for the largest and most important international centres. In the case of the UK, for example, exports of financial services go quite a way to financing the deficit in the trade of manufactured goods. For most other centres, however, the size of the financial community that they attract is too small to generate significant direct benefits for the economy as a whole.

What matters all the more are the indirect benefits generated by having access to thriving financial markets. In some product areas, such as foreign exchange, this is not the same as having a national financial centre. Firms and individuals can easily use products and services from afar. In other product areas – such as M&A, stockmarket trading, and equity issuance – access to expertise in the same location becomes crucial for the quality of services. Interestingly, it is precisely these products that matter most for macroeconomic performance. They help in the crucial task of restructuring industries, in allocating capital and in ensuring that management acts in the interests of owners and other 'stakeholders'.

4 Competitive Dynamics

The ranking of centres that emerges from Chapter 2 hardly comes as a surprise. London is the undisputed premier financial centre in the time zone. That Frankfurt consistently ranks ahead of Paris may be unexpected for some observers; it is, nonetheless, underpinned by a growing lead in a number of product areas. In the competition for the *prix de l'Euro*, Frankfurt seems to be holding more cards than its chief continental rival.[93]

Trends over time are a little more unexpected. What stands out is the extent to which London's lead appears to be lengthening. For all the speed of growth on the continent over recent years, there is no sense in which any continental rival can be said to be narrowing the gap with London in products other than those driven by domestic markets and/or infrastructure. In particular, we find that London is the only truly international centre, exporting financial services on a vast scale, while also being largely self-sufficient in satisfying the demands of domestic clients. Frankfurt, and to a lesser extent, Paris, are its major clients. Adjusted for the size of the national economies, they are amongst the most intensive users of London's services. In contrast, the exports of financial services by Frankfurt and Paris have dwindled recently, even falling in absolute value in a rapidly expanding sector of world trade. At the same time, the share of wholesale financial services in national product appears to have grown more slowly than in the UK. What accounts for these developments? And what, if anything, could continental centres do to improve their situation?

INTERPRETING THE EVOLUTION OF EUROPEAN FINANCIAL CENTRES

Criteria of Excellence

There are a few ingredients that normally should make for a successful financial centre:

- market infrastructure
- professional players
- international products
- economic environment
- regulatory conditions

Financial centres have to provide a cost-efficient market infrastructure. Market infrastructure in its wider sense refers to all rules and customs governing securities transactions and all associated businesses, directly influencing the extent to which fair and orderly markets exist in all products. However, access to markets is no longer synonymous with the physical proximity of stock exchanges and trading floors. Bond traders have long used the telephone as a primary means of negotiating trades. Electronic trading of shares and derivatives, combined with remote membership and remote clearing, has greatly reduced the need to locate in the same place as the markets themselves.

The presence of major players is vital for any international financial centre. The most immediate benefit a country can reap from becoming an attractive location for financial intermediaries lies in the employment opportunities created, profits generated, taxes paid, and the skills transferred by attracting the top securities houses, issuers and institutional investors. This core community of financial service institutions thrives on and in turn stimulates a whole plethora of auxiliary services: specialist law firms, accounting firms, head-hunters, and so on. A second group of institutions whose presence indirectly benefits financial centres are precisely those firms that use the same specialist service providers, that is, international insurance brokers, trading houses and corporate headquarters of international companies.

Attractive products are the third element without which a financial centre cannot thrive. Availability of a full range of domestic products – from blue-chip stocks to custody services, from asset management products to derivatives – is only a first step. Perhaps even more importantly, successful financial centres attract business in international benchmark products. Some centres are lucky in having domestic products that have acquired benchmark status. For a truly international centre, this factor will be largely immaterial; its other advantages are sufficient to attract significant volume in any international benchmark product, whatever its origin.[94] Also, new products should be developed at a high frequency, thus boosting the business of securities firms and attesting to the superior value added to clients' businesses.

Financial centres can profit from being located in a country with a strong, large economy. A dynamic economic environment presents special opportunities. Growth goes hand in hand with buoyant demand for financial services; the sophistication of products used by final customers is often highly correlated with their overall success. Prudent pension systems use the power of compound interest to safeguard against old-age poverty, and generate a stable demand for securities and asset management services. The absolute size of the domestic market also matters. Many of the businesses conducted in financial centres have a strong fixed-cost element. Larger markets therefore allow economies of scale to be exploited. In addition to the demand for services, the economic environment has another impact. A stable currency, an effective central bank and a strong entrepreneurial spirit will benefit the wholesale financial sector as well.

The regulatory environment has an indirect but important impact on the fortunes of financial centres. In addition to its immediate role in shaping orderly markets, almost all areas of regulatory intervention influence the competitiveness of financial centres. Labour laws and practices can act as a significant constraint; accounting standards can obscure the profitability of firms, and skewed taxation may provide incentives for inefficiency. Banking laws may favour credit provision over securities markets, and foreign trade can be stifled by quotas and tariffs.

These five elements of excellence do not have equal influence. Some factors, such as the presence of major players, access to efficient markets and attractive products, are essential to our definition of a financial centre. Elements such as regulation and the economic environment can support its development or prove a major constraint, but are insufficient by themselves to determine the fate of a financial centre. New York's role was severely affected by regulation Q and other interventions in the 1950s and 1960s, yet retained its influence on the back of its other strengths. The UK's demise as the world's leading industrial nation, and the pound's fall from major currency status, have also done little to undermine the City's international role. The presence of orderly, fair and efficient markets is a *sine qua non*. Initially, the trading of attractive foreign products and the presence of international players are signs of success, and not its cause. But domestic products with international benchmark status are not necessary for achieving an outstanding position, as the case of the UK clearly demonstrates.

The Limits of the Checklist Approach

Ten years ago, using the checklist above, it was quite easy to explain why London towered over its continental rivals. It had had a highly successful futures and options exchange in the form of LIFFE since the early 1980s. Its SEAQ system was capturing what appeared to be an ever-increasing share of trading in continental European shares. The major push in favour of deregulation, the 1986 'Big Bang', had given London a highly competitive regulatory regime. Combined with its traditional dominance in the Eurobond markets and the strength of domestic merchant banks, it was not hard to see why continental centres struggled. Germany had only just reintroduced the trading of derivatives. The levying of minimum reserve requirements on repo transactions made these prohibitively expensive. A stamp duty burdened share trading, and the fragmented nature of German stock exchanges, with Düsseldorf and Frankfurt trading very similar volumes, compounded the problem. The fairness of markets was not always ensured, giving continental centres a bad name. Corporate bond issuance on the continent was almost unknown, and IPO volumes were puny.

Ten years later, many of the regulatory barriers are gone. From minimum reserve requirements for repos to stamp duties, from the fragmented nature of share trading on the floor of numerous regional exchanges to the prohibition of derivatives trading, continental centres have made a quantum leap forward. Great strides have been made in reforming regulation, improving the fairness of markets and eliminating obstacles such as the levying of minimum reserve requirements on repo transactions. Suggestions of insider trading are largely a thing of the past.

More importantly, the infrastructure of continental centres now provides a benchmark for efficiency world-wide. Both Paris and Frankfurt adopted electronic trading early on and wholeheartedly. Implementation of the new systems went smoothly, in contrast to the Taurus débâcle suffered by London. Frankfurt's integration of clearing, equity trading, and the derivatives exchange is widely regarded as an important advantage. As a result, the quality of market infrastructure in continental centres is now at least on par with that in London. These improvements were part of a deliberate effort to promote Frankfurt and Paris as financial centres. Germany introduced a string of laws to promote financial markets (*Finanzplatzförderungsgesetze*); the financial community built up the widely respected *Finanzplatz* organization.[95] Paris has worked hard to make French debt the European benchmark, and has used Paris Europlace as a way of promoting its role as a financial centre. Pessimistic observers could now argue that these campaigns have come to nought, though this would probably be premature. To be sure, some problems remain. The Index of Economic Freedom, compiled annually by the Heritage Foundation, continues to give Germany and France bad grades for taxation, the state of their banking system (largely because of the role of state-owned banks) and, in the case of France, for the freedom of capital flows.[96] For some new products, market participants on the continent continue to complain about slow regulatory approval. However, compared with ten years ago, regulatory problems appear to be minor today.

However, the flow of talented personnel is still hindered by the high rates of income taxation in both Germany and France. Nonetheless, as some

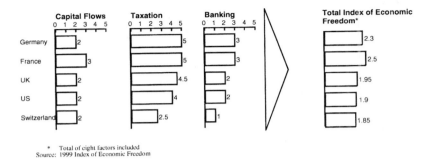

* Total of eight factors included
Source: 1999 Index of Economic Freedom

Figure 4.1   Freedom of economic conditions: capital flows, taxation and banking 1999

firms have shown, a significant local presence in high-margin markets can generate sufficient revenues to more than compensate for these higher costs.

A Different Twist to the Tale

What mainly underlies the observed trends over time are the sheer momentum of agglomeration and the law of comparative advantage. Using our list of five criteria to explain changes in the competitive position of financial centres is complicated by the self-reinforcing nature of agglomeration. Financial centres are places where major players trade benchmark products on efficient markets and provide wholesale financial services to the rest of the economy. But also, their position may strengthen because they have achieved a critical mass in terms of world-class firms and talented individuals. There appear to be increasing returns to scale in many talent-based industries. Concentration of financial services in one physical location, despite remote membership, still appears to offer sufficient rewards to offset the exorbitant rents and considerable disamenities associated with locating, for instance, in the centre of capital cities. The most common explanation is positive externalities, indirect benefits that can take a multitude of forms from opportunities for informal exchange to highly specialized auxiliary services and a flexible, deep pool of talented professionals. Concentration, then, yields considerable benefits, but also causes additional costs. The number of international financial centres will depend on how costs and benefits are balanced. The sheer momentum of the centre that is ahead today, gaining ever larger market shares because of positive externalities, makes itself felt more strongly in some markets than in others. We have already found that the leading centre in the time zone is lengthening its lead in the high-volume, low-margin businesses (where economies of scale matter) as well as in those new products that require considerable ingenuity during the early stages of development. Simply levelling the playing field through improved infrastructure and better regulation is not enough to attract international business to continental centres – just as building extra garages is not sufficient to stimulate the next Silicon Valley. Economic history is full of cases where the better product eventually lost out simply because it came later; network effects had given the products that started first a substantial advantage.[97] Proximity to clients may, however, in some areas, outweigh the benefits of an early start.

Also, countries are bound to specialize in the goods and services in which they have a relative advantage, compared with their own performance in other sectors. Absolute advantage is, in the pure Ricardian model, irrelevant. Trade is beneficial for both productive and less productive countries. Because of the basic principles of international trade, even if one country is universally superior in its productivity and competitiveness across all sectors, it would not be sensible to produce all goods on its own. By buying goods from a country that is less efficient in producing some of these goods compared with itself, and only producing (and exporting) the goods that it is best at, overall welfare increases substantially. In this sense, the dismal export performance of Germany and France in financial services is no cause for major concern; indeed, it would betray a mercantilist frame of mind to assume that strong exports should automatically be a sensible aim of policy. By specializing in its still competitive manufacturing sector, and importing financial services, Germany is probably increasing its economic well-being overall.

Also, the strong performance of the City is in part explained by the continuing decline of the UK's manufacturing industry. The weakness of the continental centres in truly international financial products is also driven by the sheer strength of their manufacturing sectors. Since manufacturing is still so much larger an industry than financial services, to speak of head-to-head competition in the latter (without paying due regard to the total dynamics of comparative advantage, instead of focusing on absolute advantage) is to think of the tail wagging the dog. Total UK manufacturing output in 1998 was barely higher than at the last peak in 1990, and productivity performance has been disappointing. While productivity per employee surged in the 1980s, it has not changed much over the last economic cycle (note, however, that capital productivity has risen substantially). Export performance is degenerating, with the trade account showing increasing deficits. Relative to the growth of its main foreign markets for manufactured goods, the UK's exports are underperforming. In 1997, the loss of market share was equivalent to 2.4 per cent; in 1998, the UK underperformed (relative to its possibilities) by a full 7.9 per cent. Germany's manufacturing sector, in contrast, outperformed its competitors, and managed to sell more abroad than was in line with the growth in these markets. In 1997, the outperformance was equivalent to 1 per cent; in 1998, it was 0.8 per cent. The French manufacturing sector also recorded gains in market share of 3.4 per cent and 0.3 per cent respectively (Figure 4.2).[98] It is, of course, debatable if Germany should really export more (in terms of value) pulp and paper than financial services. In so far as Germany's weak showing in financial service exports is simply indicative of superior productivity in the manufacturing sector as a whole, it does not contradict our argument.

If our line of reasoning is correct, what are the policy implications? First, there is an argument to be made that major financial centres have become icons of national pride and independence; desired not for immediate benefit, but also for status reasons. Politicians everywhere often seek to bask in the glory of a sophisticated, internationally competitive financial centre.[99] As our evidence shows, this is not without reason – jobs in financial services (especially in wholesale banking) are highly attractive. They are well-paid, growing in number, and an important source of tax revenue. It would be a dubious general policy to promote 'national champions' in services (as it has generally proved to be in manufacturing). Whether the loci of attention

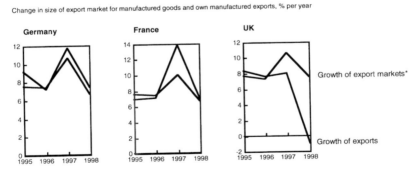

Change in size of export market for manufactured goods and own manufactured exports, % per year

* Weights based on 1994 market share
Source: OECD

Figure 4.2   Manufacturing: market growth and export performance

are geographical entities such as a city, or an individual company, is immaterial. Before such policy initiatives are questioned too much, we should add one important distinction. Financial services can be provided for clients abroad; to specialize in this particular sector may or may not make sense, depending on the sustainable competitive position in other parts of the economy.

That a country may sensibly decide not to aim for major exporter status of financial services (and hence decides to do little to boost its national financial centre's international standing) is, however, not the same as saying that it should be equally happy to purchase the vast majority of financial services abroad. Not concentrating on exports is not the same as deciding not to reduce import dependence. This is because of the nature of some financial services. We argued earlier that there are, in principle, two kinds of services – those that could, in principle, be performed anywhere (for example, forex trading), and those that benefit from proximity to clients and other locals (such as M&A). In the case of the latter, import substitution can bring benefits in so far as it raises the quality of services provided. If more vibrant national capital markets and highly professional financial services provide important advantages above and beyond those reflected in prices, policy intervention to aid the growth of the national financial services sector can yield benefits. A greater role for tradable assets enhances the liquidity of portfolios and facilitates risk management. If local firms acquire better research coverage, this may increase valuation levels and reduce the cost of finance.[100] More and better-trained M&A specialists will facilitate the restructuring and expansion of national industries and firms. Deeper national equity markets with greater liquidity will provide additional finance for firms and also furnish the benefits of investor oversight and pressure. More advanced asset management firms can help to boost returns for savers in the home market. In many of these branches of wholesale banking, greater size of the sector also means lower fees (as we have documented), reducing the burden that the financial sector imposes on the rest of the economy and increasing the use of its services. To develop the provision of these services is in the economic interest of the home country. Many European countries are now beyond the minimum threshold size that makes it viable for firms to establish local teams of specialists. It is in this sense that continental European countries have scored some remarkable successes over the last few years.

What of the future? We expect London to grow in every part of wholesale banking that is, in essence, without a natural location. 'Everybody has to be somewhere', as Spike Milligan put it.[101] In the European time zone, this somewhere is London if the economics of the business allow it to be concentrated at all. The normal externalities of concentrating human capital in one location will prevail in favour of the UK as long as its tax rates, culture and language do not stand in the way of the flow of international talent to its shores. It is in these truly globalized product areas that London will, in all likelihood, continue to gain market share. The UK's role as a financial centre may well continue to thrive on the back of a declining and uncompetitive manufacturing sector, because it is being pushed to emphasize one of its remaining areas of strength.

At the same time, London appears to be losing some of its role as a hub for European markets. In the businesses that are multi-local by their very nature, centrifugal tendencies appear to be winning slowly. These are areas with considerable value added. The benefits of informal exchange, better markets for talented professionals and greater specialization are insufficient to outweigh the advantages of continuous close contact with local clients and a richer understanding of national economic, legal and cultural conditions.

COULD CONTINENTAL CENTRES COMPETE?

Wholesale banking products fall into two main categories: inherently local business and truly international products. Essentially local business requires an extensive presence in the location where business originates. Examples are M&A, analyst coverage and, to a lesser extent, bond and equity underwriting. Specialists in these areas need not reside permanently in the same country where the business is conducted, but their physical presence is required for longer periods. At the other end of the spectrum, businesses such as forex or bond trading can more or less be conducted from any location on the globe. Decisions about where to locate are largely driven by costs and regulations as well as access to infrastructure. The increasing availability of remote access has added to the range of products in the latter category of essentially 'homeless' products. Location is also less of an issue in new products that have just been invented; it may be no accident where a particular product was first designed, but given the fact that volumes are still small and the number of specialists limited, decisions about location are still malleable.

Local Business – High Margins, Moderate to High Volumes, High Growth

As capital markets in continental Europe mature and companies begin to use securities for their funding needs, growth rates in M&A, equity under-

writing, and so on, have been impressive. Not all of the business generated
on the continent is actually served by local experts. Inherently, however,
the nature of the business requires a considerable amount of physical
presence; beyond a minimum threshold, most players decide to establish a
local presence. Value added per head in this business is high, providing good
jobs and attractive profits. Total value added accruing locally is determined
by local market size and the percentage of local business served by local
staff. In most continental countries, local market size has shown significant
growth and is shaping up to compete with UK volumes. The proportion of
business retained by domestic financial centres, in contrast, has been the
main constraint. Determining factors here are local tax rates, as well as the
normal set of locational necessities for expatriate communities.

International Business – Plain Vanilla

There are several high-volume, low-margin products in wholesale banking:
forex trading, bond trading and the trading of some futures and options.
Volume growth may still be strong, but the profitability of the business as
a whole has been subject to considerable pressure over the last years. Within
Europe – and often on a world-wide scale – London towers over its rivals
in precisely these businesses. Key factors of success in these businesses are
regulatory cost and liquidity. There is precious little reason to try to compete
in these areas. First, it is unlikely that continental centres will be able to
draw sufficient business for this to be viable, since they lack liquidity, and
in the absence of exogenous shocks, stand little chance to attract it. Second,
the business itself is not sufficiently attractive to warrant a major effort.

International Business – Rising Stars

Many of the more recent innovations in financial products still show low
volumes, but high growth rates and attractive margins. Credit derivatives,
energy trading and European high-yield products are prominent examples.
Most of the business in these areas is located in London, where many of
the initial inventions were made. Costs are much less of an issue in these
products; what matters much more is access to a large pool of talented
individuals who can turn an idea into a profitable product, as well as sophisticated customers who are willing to put new ideas to the test. Not all of
these products will necessarily turn into multibillion-dollar businesses, but
some will. Acquiring this set of growth options has value above and beyond
the revenues, taxes and salaries generated in the beginning. Once these

products have matured, liquidity and access to a much larger pool of talent become decisive; their 'stickiness' increases as revenues begin to pour in.

A Strategy for the Second Tier?

Fee levels in many product areas are healthy in continental Europe, but total volumes have not caught up with the UK. At the same time, the amount of business generated is increasing rapidly. As a result, total revenues generated in Frankfurt and Paris may – for some products – even overtake the UK. It is unlikely that such conditions will last indefinitely. Fee levels will come under increasing pressure as competition increases and the sophistication of customers grows. In the long run, total revenue is likely to stagnate or perhaps even fall, as further volume growth is unlikely to compensate fully for the fall in fees.

This implies that there may be a window of opportunity for second-tier financial centres in Europe, like Frankfurt and Paris. This is because of the importance of externalities for the competition between European financial centres. Both the concentration of talent as well as of liquidity tend to be sticky; historical accident matters in determining future competitiveness in truly international businesses. The aim therefore has to be to increase the domestic capture of business generated at home and add to the stock of expertise in the domestic centre during the initial phase of good growth and high fee levels. While this momentum in terms of new staff and reputation continues, second-tier centres can also try to gain a toehold in the most promising areas of future growth. Given the externalities involved, temporary subsidies would be needed to align incentives. This appears to be one of the few ways in which Europe's second-tier financial centres can begin to capture truly international business. Whether the rewards are sufficient to balance the costs is another matter.

Summary

It had already been argued that it may not be sensible for continental centres to compete head-on with London in many areas in which it enjoys such a commanding lead. In addition to the dubious economic benefits – it is not clear that the financial service sector enjoys any absolute or comparative advantage in most continental European countries – it may also be impractical and imprudent to compete in any of the high-volume, truly globalized product areas. First, these are not very attractive to begin with. In forex, for example, in many ways the most typical example in this category, margins are wafer-thin already, and many houses are reducing their head-count in this area. Second, the differences in size and the benefits of agglomeration are sufficiently large to make it highly unlikely that competing with London could yield anything but the most paltry of results. The importance of agglomeration economics are such that historical accidents (such as London's nineteenth-century role) may still echo in its vast lead in many product areas.

The question posed whether it is more important for the national economic welfare to have a financial centre, or to have access to superior financial services provided by a foreign centre. In the products where economies of scale are of almost exclusive importance, mercantilist policies that try to promote financial services exports will not pay for the centres that are currently behind. Just as in the case of stock exchanges, where trading is subject to large economies of scale, but listings, and so on are not, there is nonetheless an important role to be played by domestic financial service sectors. Local products produced locally can be tailored to the needs of local clients, and prices will inevitably fall as the industry matures. The important externalities and benefits that capital market-based financial systems offer can be enhanced by developing these local industries. Only in selected product areas, where economies of scale are important in principle, but – due to the underdeveloped state of the market – have not asserted themselves fully, should second-tier financial centres such as Paris and Frankfurt hope to gain market share in international business.

THE EURO AND THE CITY – A BURNING NON-ISSUE?

Much ink has been spilled over the likely impact of the euro's introduction on the competition of financial centres. Some in the UK feared that remaining outside monetary union would prejudice London's chances severely, and that Paris and Frankfurt would be likely to gain at its expense. The Lord Mayor of the City of London, Lord Levene, suggested as much when he said before a gathering of financial service professionals: 'A significant number of responsible and acute observers in Europe believe that London's business would, in time, be eroded if the UK's entry into EMU is long delayed.'[102] In practice, the impact appears to have been very limited.

Expectations before the Launch of EMU

The argument in favour of such a major shift in competitive positions rested on three considerations. First, a more general argument about the development of European capital markets was being made. Once the euro created a large, unified pool of investable funds, and firms were waking up to the opportunities of tapping this market, more of the capital market business would automatically migrate to continental centres. Given that continental economies still record a relatively limited use of equity and bonds, compared with the size of their GDP, the scope for future growth would be considerable. Critical mass for placing teams of specialists could easily be reached; consequently, London would lose market share. Eventually, due to the greater attractions of Euroland's capital markets, a high proportion of business denominated in euros would be transacted within the EMU area.[103]

The second argument focused on Target, the real-time gross settlement (RTGS) system for large-scale transfers in euros. Every EMU member country can make full use of Target, including access to overnight liquidity. The UK, in contrast, is only allowed use of the payment function. UK-domiciled banks have to close all positions by the end of the business day. The argument against full access was that, otherwise, money creation would partly be in the hands of a non-EMU country. It was widely feared that this refusal to allow full Target access would disadvantage the City, increasing the cost of funds. Some observers argued that trading-related business was bound to suffer.

Third, the decision to locate the European Central Bank (ECB) in Frankfurt was seen as an important scoop that would boost its role as a financial centre. With monetary policy being decided on the continent, market-watchers and the traders and support staff who depend on getting an early impression of likely developments would have to move, possibly taking other specialists with them.

The Impact of EMU

Many predictions made about the impact of the euro on European capital markets appear to have come to pass. The euro has had the expected effect of creating a much larger, integrated capital market at a stroke for some products. The effect is felt most acutely in the bond markets. Issuance of corporate paper, long virtually unknown in Europe, rose rapidly in 1999. Most spectacularly, the euro 6.25 bn financing for Olivetti's takeover of Telecom Italia created a big precedent. Emerging market issuers have flocked to the euro as a currency of issue, partly driven by interest rates that were lower than for dollar-denominated paper.

At the same time, many of the pessimistic predictions about the City's future role have been proven wrong. Neither Target nor the deepening of Europe's capital markets appears to have had a sizeable impact. In practice, very few banks even in the pre-EMU RTGSs kept positions open overnight. The Bank of England (BoE) has also offered to keep a sufficient amount of euros available for payments purposes. At present, it keeps euro 3 bn in its Target account with the ECB, which can be used for payments by UK-based banks. The cost to UK is no more than the interest forgone on euro 3 bn. Note that the cost is relatively small; since overnight positions are heavily discouraged, the Bank deposits euros every morning, and withdraws them late in the evening to lend overnight. There is no access to overnight liquidity, which carries a penalty of 500 bp over the ECB lending rate for 'out' participants. However, for most houses, payments can easily be handled through continental subsidiaries. As a result, UK securities firms have access to euro liquidity on more or less identical terms with the rest of the EMU area. For payments within the UK, they can simply use the familiar CHAPS system, which offers a separate facility for dealing in euros. From the start of monetary union, 20 banks became settlement members, and some 330 became indirect participants.[104] Immediately after the introduction of the new currency, it was handling some euro 140 bn in transactions per day.[105]

The ECB's move to Frankfurt, for all its symbolic quality in ensuring continuity with the Bundesbank, also did little to attract additional members to the investment banking community. This is for two reasons. First, the logic of expecting the actual physical location of the central bank to gain significantly was always flawed: 'US banks have not moved down to Washington to watch the Federal Reserve Board; they can do that perfectly well from New York.'[106] Second, the ECB is easily one of the most secretive central banks anywhere. From the refusal to publish minutes in a timely fashion to the secrecy surrounding internal discussions, the ECB gives securities houses precious little reason to try to catch every rumour and casual comment by its officials – because there are so precious few of them.

The issuance of European corporate and high-yield bonds at last appears to be taking off – but it is largely managed out of London. Issuance volume in euros in the first five months of 1999 alone was almost double that in all the currencies of the 11 member states in the whole of 1998.[107] However, there is no way in which the introduction of the euro has somehow suspended or modified the 'rules of the game'. Many of the infrastructure providers in London have long been capable of handling multiple currencies; for example, trading shares denominated in euros was not a major step for the London Stock Exchange, which before 1999 was already handling transactions in nine currencies. Continental European financial centres now often continue to trade in only one currency – only it is the euro. When it comes to trading bonds and equities, or doing research on these products, London has also already gained from the introduction of the euro. Whereas bonds and equity traders and research teams often used to be organized along geographical lines, with specialists covering French OATs, say, the introduction of the euro has triggered considerable reorganization. For instance, much of the organization of equities trading is now done along sectoral lines. In bonds, staff specialize in maturities, not country of origin. The single currency thus reinforces the trends caused by risk-management considerations, which make it advisable to concentrate all positions in one book. As Simon Bunce, managing director of interest-rate products at Warburg Dillon Read, put it: 'Local sales teams can be helpful in servicing a broad client base. But a regional trading presence is a relic from formerly domestic focused markets and does not add value in a single-currency environment.'[108] In 1995, nearly all equity portfolios of institutional investors for Europe were organized by country. By 1999, 64 per cent had moved to a sectoral approach.[109] The consequence of these changes is that many securities firms concentrate their specialists in one geographical location. This 'means we ... trade all the countries off the same desk. And the obvious place to do that is here', says Charles Berman of Salomon Smith Barney in London.[110]

One area in which the advent of EMU could have marked off a discontinuity was in the trading of derivatives products. Short-term interest-rate products had remained an area of strength for London's LIFFE, even after the benchmark Bund contract had been lost to Eurex. Initially, LIFFE backed euro Libor as a successor to its highly successful DM Libor future. In contrast, Eurex was betting on a Euribor-based product, based on a reference interest rate compiled on the basis of information provided by a wider range of banks. Within days, it was clear that the market favoured Euribor over euro Libor; yet instead of business migrating to the continental exchanges, LIFFE simply converted its existing contract. As a result, it lost only a small fraction of its market share.

Policy Implications

Should the UK eventually join EMU, it may have few benefits for the City. Access to Target on fully equal terms will have next to no effect. There is also only limited reason to expect that exchange-based trading would migrate to London, or a larger share of issuance would be conducted there. What determines London's standing was recently summed up by Rolf Breuer, CEO of Deutsche Bank and chairman of the German Stock Exchange: 'London will no doubt remain the leading centre in Europe thanks to its advantages of size, excellently qualified personnel, and the attractive tax, legal and cultural environment.' It is therefore no surprise that Deutsche is putting its money where its mouth is, spending an estimated US$500 mn on a new international investment banking head-quarters in London.

If the upside for the City from the UK joining the euro is limited, the potential downside is not. London is an offshore centre in more ways than one. It is less integrated into the European capital market than other centres, and is fighting hard to retain the offshore advantages in many of its businesses (see, for example, the recent discussion about a withholding tax on interest paid out on Eurobonds). The flexibility of its regulatory regime has been crucial for the City's success. Until recently, multiple institutions were responsible for regulating different parts of the financial services sector, encouraging close co-operation between regulators and market par-ticipants, and permitting flexible arrangements in new markets. The new FSA could easily use its formidable powers to turn this light regulatory touch into a tight grip. It is therefore interesting to note that one of its objectives is to protect 'innovation and international competitiveness' in the City, a requirement that has no match in any of the statutes for regulators on the continent.[111] Joining EMU may eventually imperil this, as continental bankers continue to prefer interventionist mechanisms that can severely disrupt markets, such as the (interest-free) minimum reserve that the Bundesbank long levied, effectively driving the repo market away.

SUMMARY: LIMITS TO COMPETITION BETWEEN FINANCIAL CENTRES

The competitive metaphor is a powerful one. Many an article about London, Frankfurt and Paris as financial centres deliberately invokes the imagery of the Wild West. Indeed, 'Dueling Markets' was the title of a recent piece.[112] Before too many settlement specialists start whistling Ennio Morricone's tunes on their way to work, it is important to stress that to speak of countries and financial centres as competing in the same way as companies is to distort the case. As we have argued above, many of the changes we observe are best interpreted as a consequence of comparative advantage and agglomeration economics – and not as a case of 'High Noon'. This implies that it is better for Europe to have one truly international financial centre, instead of a string of also-rans, and that everybody's welfare is enhanced if – in the most globalized product areas – trading, product development and execution are heavily concentrated in one location. Where this one location is matters little, as long as there is easy access to cheap, reliable, innovative financial services everywhere. Services in general come in two flavours:

those that are inherently local in nature, and those that, once produced, can be used anywhere, anytime. The former are all the typical products of the service economy, such as restaurant meals or taxi rides. The quality of staff training, attention to detail, a powerful brand and face-to-face contact with consumers are key factors of success. In the latter type, such as software, the same product can be used anywhere on the globe, independent of where it has been produced. What separates success and failure is the user-friendliness, reliability or the novelty of the product. In truly global products, the nature of financial services is much closer to the Hollywood model than, say, the services offered by medical doctors. And in the same way as there is only one truly global film industry, the natural number of financial centres may well be small.

Perhaps more importantly, for these products, the location of the 'campuses' can also only be influenced to a very limited extent. Levelling the playing field alone will not lead to a more dispersed distribution of talents, securities houses or market shares in the truly global products. It is in this sense that the competitive metaphor is of limited value. The normal benefits of competition, such as lower prices or faster innovation, do not exist if there are increasing returns to concentration. The natural and most efficient outcome may well be a monopoly, that is, simply one international financial centre per time zone.

But regulatory initiatives and improvements in market infrastructure do have a role to play. Not all financial services can be produced without a significant local component, as they are more similar to the work of medical doctors than to the products of film stars and starlets. M&As and IPOs need to be adapted to individual needs, and the service needs to be provided in accordance with local cultural preferences and legal traditions and within the regulatory framework set by national laws. In these product areas, the benefits of agglomeration may not be negligible, either, but they are outweighed by the benefits of tailoring a product to suit local demand. Domestic teams of specialists operating from the national centre will develop once a minimum size of market is reached. Again, the limits of the competitive metaphor are apparent: having a larger number of M&A origination specialists in Paris does not diminish London's role. Instead of fighting over the share of the pie, such a shift increases its size overall, and certainly raises the quality.

To abandon hopes for a global financial centre may hurt national pride, just as the decline or closure of numerous regional stock exchanges incensed local politicians all over Europe during the 1980s and 1990s. However, clear-headed politicians will realize that the pain is limited. What emerged most clearly in Chapter 3 was that their direct benefits, in terms of value added locally and the employment created, are very small for all except the most dominant financial centres. Strikingly, they appear particularly small in the most globalized product areas, where today's dominant centres have the edge. Far more important are the indirect benefits that flow from access to world-class financial services, wherever they are produced. Nor does this necessarily relegate second-tier financial centres to stagnation and mediocrity. Many of the jobs they create are in the most attractive businesses of all, with fast growth, high margins and good employment creation. Moreover, it is through the wider provision of these services that many of Europe's sclerotic economies can receive effective treatment of their most pressing ailments. Restructuring and an increased role for markets – especially equity markets – can do much to revive the flagging fortunes of corporatist economies.[113] Some steps that may be worth taking are discussed below.

London's Last Laugh: A Speculation

It appears that London's lead is unlikely to be eroded in the near future. In many products from asset management to forex, from OTC derivatives to bond issuance, its position is strong and improving. In most businesses, as noted above, London still has approximately five times the number of employees of Frankfurt or Paris. The strongest reason for London's dominance, we argued, is no longer any palpable structural or regulatory advantage, but the simple momentum of a centre that is already ahead of the rest. In an industry where agglomeration itself yields considerable benefits, the accident of being first may also perpetuate itself. At the same time, change is not necessarily continuous, and the rules of the game may change quickly. When Irving Fisher, Professor of Economics at Yale University, observed in 1929 that 'stocks have reached what looks like a permanently high plateau', he was not making an off-the-cuff remark, but, as one of the foremost economic minds of his generation, was summarizing some of his thoughts. If it is so easy even for the most informed judges to be so wrong in retrospect, where could we have made a mistake? Or, put another way, what scenarios can we imagine that would change the current situation significantly, triggering a precipitous shift?

The analogy used most often in this context is that of grains of sand, being slowly added to a small sandpile. Initially, each grain of sand makes little difference, except to increase the height of the pile by a fraction. When the angle becomes too steep, however, the final grain causes an avalanche that restores the normal pyramid shape. The lesson, of course, is that change need not be continuous, and that small and steady shifts can in the end lead to major discontinuities. From price changes (which are often too extreme compared with the bell curve) to the role of individual firms (take the rise and fall of Salomon, for example), financial markets have had their fair share of such changes.

Derivatives trading may be the most relevant analogy. Liquidity in a market shares many characteristics with the externalities generated by agglomeration; again, those who are first have been dealt a better deck of cards. It was long thought that electronic derivatives markets, whatever their cost advantages, would never be able to compete effectively with traditional pit markets. After all the biggest cost associated with trading tends to be price impact (the extent to which the market price moves against the buyer/seller), and not fees. In other words, traditional markets could offer the smallest price impact of big trades, thus compensating for their antiquated trading mechanism. In this fashion, they would remain cost-competitive – or so people thought. When David Kynaston published his history of LIFFE in 1996, there was apparently no reason why things should ever change.[114] Using traditional pit trading methods, LIFFE dominated trading in short-term interest-rate products as well as futures on gilts, Italian government debt and, most importantly, the Bund, the world's most active financial derivatives contract. Despite being challenged by the Deutsche Terminbörse (DTB) since 1989, LIFFE had managed to retain a vastly superior market share in the Bund. All through 1997, Eurex (the result of a

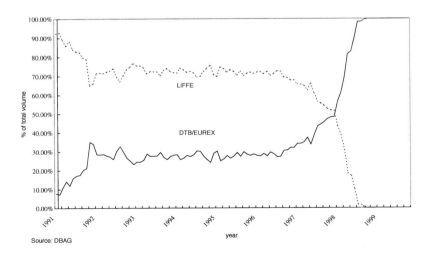

Figure 4.3   Market shares in the Bund future, 1998

merger between DTB and Soffex) gained ground. Gradually, as Eurex volume rose at the expense of LIFFE, the odds began to shift. Then, in 1998, over a period of six months, LIFFE's market share went from close to 50 per cent to less than 10 per cent.

What, if anything, could have a similar impact on the size and importance of financial centres? Leaving on one side entirely unlikely eventualities such as war and plague, there are three main possibilities.

First, a political backlash against freer markets. Since the UK records very high rates of equity exposure, with many people having taken out endowment mortgages, where repayment partly depends on the performance of asset markets, a crash in the stockmarket would leave many people short-changed. Given the interventionist outlook of many in the ruling Labour Party, a political sea-change as a result of declining equity markets cannot be ruled out completely. At the moment, the FSA is a standard-bearer of free, open and fair markets. It is widely admired for the quality of its staff and its commitment to the light regulatory touch that, in the past, has attracted important new products such as credit derivatives to the City. Given the FSA's sweeping powers, however, it could easily be used to stifle capital markets and rein in 'excesses'.[115] Even countries such as the US with a robust free-market ideology have engaged in forms of meddling – such as in the case of regulation Q, which created the euromarkets in London – that drove business away. Such a reversal of the regulatory differences between the continent and the UK would surely do much to strengthen Paris, and also, and especially, Frankfurt.

Second, it is conceivable that changes in the regulatory regime – that is, through revisions of the Basle accord or through national rules, which can always be tougher – might dramatically increase the cost of trading. Since banks already have to put a fair amount of risk capital up for proprietary positions, any change would strongly affect the bottom line. London would be hardest hit, given its strengths in relatively capital-intensive, trading-oriented parts of the business. It is not hard to speculate about events that could trigger such a crack-down on investment banks' trading strategies. Any meltdown in the markets similar to the 1998 Russian/Asian crisis, if it is severe enough, will inevitably encourage agitation in favour of curtailing speculators. London's dominance in asset management would not be in any danger, however. Combined with the gradual melting away of London's role as a hub for execution teams, however, significant changes in the shares of value added and employment would almost certainly follow.

The third danger is in many ways the most realistic. The scenario is based on the same mechanism as the second discontinuity. There are many factors favouring the current trend towards integration of investment banks with retail brokerages, and mergers with commercial banks are increasingly common. From the Morgan Stanley/Dean Witter Discovery link-up to Merrill Lynch, the industry is increasingly convinced that investment banking without strong in-house distribution to retail customers is not the *modus operandi* of the future. After the repeal of the Glass-Steagall Act (with its provisions to keep commercial and investment banking separate), this trend is sure to accelerate. Many of the new, integrated firms view trading activities with much more suspicion than do investment banks, and commercial bankers often seize the commanding heights. Salomon's trading activities, for example, were severely curtailed after the Travellers/Citibank merger. A more sceptical approach by an increasing number of financial conglomerates and universal banks that dominate the investment-banking industry will also shift the industry to locations that are less trading-driven than London. The true charm of the businesses that Frankfurt – and, to a lesser extent, Paris – have attracted is that they require little capital, produce good revenues per employee and hold out the promise of rapid future growth. An investment-banking industry that has largely fallen into the hands of universal banks, facing a downturn in the markets and a corresponding collapse in proprietary trading profits, may well decide that these are the right businesses to focus on.

The UK's mighty textiles and motorcar industries all but disappeared over the last 40 years, and Germany's eminence in the natural sciences, paramount until the 1920s, is no longer even a shadow of its former self. Funny things do happen, and they may happen to financial markets as well. The possibilities we mentioned may not come to pass; or we may have overlooked the most likely eventualities. For all the impressive momentum that London shows at the moment, the future may yet hold some surprises.

5 Policy Recommendations

The competitive dynamics discussed in this book show that continental countries would benefit if they tried first to develop their own domestic markets and do what is possible to serve them well, which for many products means to serve them from a local base. Aiming for major competitor status with a significant market share in the most competitive and globalized product areas may not be feasible or, indeed, sensible. Second, continental countries might concentrate also on products that are still in their infancy, and for which their financial sectors should have a healthy appetite (such as credit derivatives, or junk bonds). A number of initiatives suggest themselves that may simultaneously strengthen domestic wholesale markets and facilitate growth and wealth creation in the economy at large.

'PRUDENT MAN' REGULATION FOR EUROPE

The importance of retirement saving for today's working population can hardly be exaggerated. The size of the demographic imbalances that is building up undermines the viability of today's pay-as-you-go systems. Obtaining high returns on retirement assets is all the more important if present consumption is not to suffer. It is therefore particularly problematic that the approach chosen to regulate institutional investments in continental Europe, which imposes largely arbitrary limits on asset classes, tends to depress asset returns. Instead, it would be more appropriate to adopt a different and more liberal approach – the so-called 'prudent man' regulation.

Two Approaches to Investment Regulation

There are essentially two approaches to investment regulation: 'prudent man' regulation, or pre-set limits on asset classes. The vast majority of continental European countries allow pension funds and insurance companies to invest only a certain percentage of their assets in, for example, equities or foreign assets. Limits such as these are intended to reduce the risk faced by investors. The other approach strives to reduce the risk for customers, but does so without strict numerical limits. Instead of limits, investment companies can conduct their business as any 'prudent man' would.

This woolly-sounding phrase is, in practice, well-defined. Nobody could claim to act in line with the principles obeyed by any prudent investor in the street when investing, say, 80 per cent of a portfolio in Russian bonds. So in essence it relies on the legal process should anything go wrong.

Realized Returns

On average, over the years 1980–93, pension funds in countries with 'prudent man' regulation returned 9.5 per cent per year, whereas those in countries with asset restrictions yielded 6.7 per cent.[116] These differences are not small. Assume that a 30-year-old man aims to retire with a nest-egg equivalent to ten times after-tax earnings. To achieve this aim, when investing in pension funds subject to asset restrictions, he would have to save 11.2 per cent of his income; under 'prudent man' regulation, he would only have to save 6.7 per cent. The difference of 4.5 per cent of his after-tax income can be consumed year after year without reducing the level of his retirement assets. For the average German production worker, 4.5 per cent of after-tax earnings would be equivalent to DM225 per month. Note also that the returns achieved by institutional investors – even those hamstrung by asset restrictions – are far higher than those achieved by private investors for their wealth as a whole.

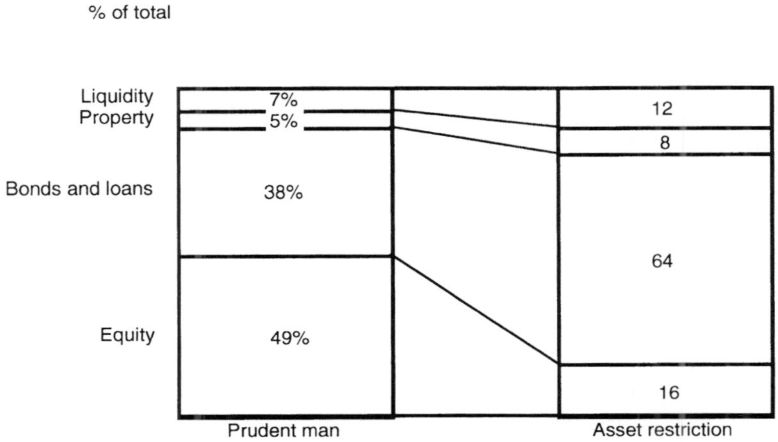

Source: EFRP

Figure 5.1   Division of assets, by category

The main reason why realized returns are considerably higher under 'prudent man' regulation is that pension funds hold higher shares of equity. Whereas in 1996 only 16 per cent of total assets in countries with restrictions were held as equities, countries with 'prudent man' regulation showed an average of 49 per cent (Figure 5.1). Bond holdings constituted another 38 per cent of the total, compared with 64 per cent in countries with asset restrictions. Also, liquidity was much lower. As this is the asset with the lowest returns, the difference of 5 percentage points on this count alone imposes a direct and considerable cost on fund holders. Finally, since there will be a lower proportion of foreign assets, opportunities for diversification go unused in countries with asset restrictions. Volatility in countries with 'prudent man' regulation is somewhat higher; but given that pension funds, by their very nature, are designed to invest for the long term, this should not be taken as an indication that 'prudent man' regulation leads to unacceptable risk levels.

Necessary Steps

Abolishing asset class restrictions in continental European countries should be relatively easy. Investors in Germany and France in particular have traditionally favoured bonds and cash over equity; it could be argued that governments would merely be ensuring that the revealed preferences of domestic investors are safeguarded. If European governments are reluctant to scrap asset class restrictions altogether, they should allow their citizens to explicitly opt out of the regulations imposed on institutional investors. The gullible and unsophisticated will automatically be protected against any increase in risk. For those who accept it in exchange for the vastly superior returns that come from asset management under 'prudent man' regulation, the possibility to opt out of over-protective clauses is a simple and elegant way to circumvent cumbersome regulations.

The alternative, a comprehensive shift in regulatory regime, could also be undertaken. Canada used to operate under asset restrictions until 1987; their abolition and the introduction of 'prudent man' regulation was not accompanied by public concern, and there have been no examples of excessive risk-taking behaviour.

Institutional investors have a particularly attractive value proposition to make in countries where the wider investing public is relatively unsophisticated, because the potential gain in realized returns is considerable. Continental countries, in particular, urgently need their populations to begin not only saving, but investing for a financially secure retirement that the state can no longer guarantee. At the moment, institutional investors cannot offer their services to the full in those areas where they are needed the most, that is, investing in rather more risky assets. Introducing 'prudent man' regulation, either as an opt-out clause or directly by abolishing asset restrictions, would be an important step towards safeguarding the financial well-being of continental Europeans in retirement.

HIGH RETURNS – JUNK BONDS, GOING PRIVATE AND A EUROPEAN TAKEOVER CODE

At the height of the takeover boom in the 1980s, a very substantial share of Fortune 500 firms were stalked by corporate predators. The market for junk bonds was instrumental in the restructuring of corporate America during the 1980s and 1990s. Mike Milken's invention of junk bonds, securities that were rated below investment-grade at the time of issuance, allowed even small takeover specialists to take on industrial giants of the size of RJR Nabisco. The second contributing factor was the relatively permissive regulatory (and cultural) environment, which allowed takeovers to proceed without political meddling and economies to be realized through divestitures, lay-offs and plant closures.

Since the 1980s, the nature of the high-yield market in the US has changed. Instead of being primarily a vehicle for funding takeovers, it is now often used by young start-up firms to raise funds they could otherwise not obtain (a role in which it had been more prominent before the 1980s merger wave). Most banks vary their lending rates only to a limited extent, and prefer to turn potentially bad risks away rather than charge them the required interest rate plus an appropriate risk premium. Such firms' ability to issue junk bonds is an alternative to equity financing – and can often lower their cost of capital.

In Europe the high-yield market is still in its infancy, but growing rapidly. Going private is difficult for legal reasons, despite considerable interest from buyout firms. A number of measures could help to accelerate the market's growth. Before we can examine them, we should briefly discuss the economic importance of active takeover markets. The second aspect, funding for high risk start-ups, is in much less need of explanation. While this can be seen as a useful aim in its own right, the development of an active takeover market depends on more than access to high-yield paper. We offer some observations on the necessary changes.

Effects of an Active Takeover Market

Takeovers do not always receive the most favourable treatment in the press, and indeed the title of the book *Barbarians at the Gate*, about KKR's raid on Nabisco, sums up many people's attitude.[117] Corporate raiders who recklessly strip and sell the assets of successful companies, fire staff, close down research and development (R&D) departments and make off with millions more robbed than earned are frequently the themes. Many of the facts, however, point in a different direction. There is now abundant evidence that the pre-bid performance of targets in hostile takeovers is indeed disappointing. Not only are existing shareholders harmed by feeble returns. Perhaps more surprisingly, the employment record of firms subject to hostile and friendly bids is also below the industry average by a substantial margin.[118] Quite simply, firms that are taken over or faced with bids have often hurt all stakeholders. Friendly takeovers of course also affect firms that have disappointed all parties concerned. Unlike the hostile takeovers, however, such firms usually operate in fundamentally healthy sectors with high rates of growth.

The main effect of takeovers, then, is to remove incompetent and/or wasteful management. Instead of relying on supervisory boards and the influence of creditors to align the interests of shareholders and managers, takeovers act as a very immediate disciplining device. In the US, an average of 7–11 per cent of all CEOs change jobs each year. In firms that have been taken over, the figure is 42 per cent in the year of the change in ownership itself; in the following year, another 19 per cent go. In more than 50 per cent of all cases, the reason cited is poor performance. Management turnover in firms that have been taken over is particularly high in those firms where performance was poorest. In many cases, the operating performance of firms subsequently improves. In 59 per cent of all cases, assets were sold; in nearly one out of five instances, some operations were shut down completely. Within three years of the takeover, profitability is up considerably.[119]

In the US, some states permit multibank holding companies (MBHCs) to operate, and others prohibit them. Takeovers are only possible in the former. Interestingly, there is conclusive evidence to suggest that profitability and total returns to shareholders are considerably higher in those US states that permit an active market for corporate control in the banking sector (by allowing MBHCs, and so on). The indirect effects of such a market at the national level are also highlighted by contrasting the years 1984–8, when the US takeover market was unusually active, with the period 1989–93, when deals were few and far between. The number of hostile takeovers plummeted by 75 per cent, from 167 to 43. During the active takeover period, management turnover and corporate performance – in terms of returns to shareholders and profitability – were highly correlated. Once the takeover frenzy had subsided due to a combination of lower valuations and an increasing use of 'poison-pill' defences, incompetent (or plain unlucky) managers were much less likely to be replaced.[120]

The changes in corporate performance therefore suggest that an active takeover market can have two main benefits. First, it acts as a measure of last resort to remove incompetent management. For all the criticisms of KKR, *Barbarians at the Gate* also detailed the extreme waste that characterized much of Nabisco's top management. Second, management in unaffected firms is disciplined by the possibility of takeovers, that is, discipline and monitoring are essential (see Box 5.1).

Box 5.1
The threat of takeover as a disciplining device

Most studies of the effects of takeovers examine either the pre-bid performance of targets, or changes in operating performance and returns to shareholders for target and acquirer once a deal has been completed – or failed. This is a rather imperfect way of examining the indirect consequences of an active takeover market. Mikkelson and Partch's study about the extent to which turnover and performance were correlated in the US in the period 1984–93 takes a first step towards rectifying this.[121]

A more sophisticated and in many ways more convincing approach has recently been pioneered in the UK. Takeover bids do not hit firms randomly. They are systematically associated with a set of observable characteristics. However, only some of these firms will actually be affected by corporate control measures. In dividing *ex post* the sample into firms that were taken over (or faced bids), and those that were not affected, the second group will contain firms that may well have faced a high risk of takeover *ex ante*. Some of the decisions by management may have been affected significantly by the threat of corporate control measures alone. In separate studies, Nuttall and Bond et al. pursue a two-step approach, examining the performance of over 600 UK non-financial firms over the period 1989–96.[122] First, they estimate the probability of a takeover using a number of exogenous variables such as company age, stockmarket-wide takeover activity, capital structure, the stage of the business cycle and performance measures. To examine the effect of takeovers, they distinguish between firms that *ex ante* appear to face a higher likelihood of control measures, instead of using actual changes to stratify the sample.

The results are broadly in line with the main findings for the US. Total factor productivity (TFP) increases with the likelihood of a takeover; in the case of hostile bids, the effect is less pronounced. Nuttall finds that a 1 standard deviation increase in the risk of takeovers (approximately 5 per cent higher takeover probability) raises TFP by 7 percentage points – a very considerable effect. Investment is often curtailed, lending some support to those who claim that an active takeover market might favour short-termism. It should be borne in mind that lower investment outlays may boost TFP, and may partly be responsible for the higher capital productivity achieved by the UK. Firms in danger of being taken over also sometimes increase their dividend payments, especially when there is a greater likelihood of hostile bids. In sum, these new findings emphasize the extent to which an active market for corporate control enhances the competitiveness of firms by indirect as well as by direct means.

Forces Favouring a European High-yield Market

It seems inevitable that corporate investment financing will become increasingly based on capital markets. As a result, the high-yield market will also grow. Two main factors can be cited. First, households are more and more taking their savings out of banks and putting them into the hands of institutional investors such as life insurance companies and mutual fund managers. In Germany, the share of deposits held with banks declined from 56.5 per cent of savings in the 1960s to 32.8 per cent in the 1990s.[123] In the US, their share declined from 35 per cent in the early 1980s to little over 20 per cent today.[124] With this disappearance of cheap funding, banks are finding it increasingly difficult to maintain their margins. The return on assets of continental banks ranges between a mere 0.08 per cent (Switzerland) to 0.61 per cent (Spain), whereas US and UK banks generate returns of 1.11 per cent and 0.78 per cent respectively. Low-volume, low-margin lending for medium-sized firms will be first on the list of business to be reduced when continental banks begin to redress the problem of paltry returns, being saddled with single-digit rates of return on equity (while US and UK banks turn in rates of 15 per cent or higher).[125] Prospects for future growth in the high-yield market appear promising. According to a survey by Merrill Lynch, only 12 per cent of the proceeds of European high-yield issues are used to refinance bank debt, whereas the corresponding figure in the US is 40 per cent. As pressure on banks' balance sheets continues, it seems likely that a higher proportion of high-yield deals will be used to pay off bank loans.

Perhaps most importantly, the need for restructuring amongst Europe's corporations is palpable. From the Telecom Italia deal to the BNP/Paribas/SocGen battle, M&As appear high on the agenda; even if not all of them require high-yield bonds, volumes will be driven up by such transactions. For instance, Tecnost, the Olivetti subsidiary that was responsible for financing the takeover, issued A3-rated bonds (Moody's; BBB+ in the S&P rating scheme). Already, 39 per cent of the proceeds of high-yield transactions are used for leveraged buyouts (LBOs). By August

1999, the total volume of LBOs already exceeded US$12 bn, with one-third of the volume being accounted for in June alone.

The introduction of the euro has helped boost this market in two important ways. First, it provides access to a much larger capital market, where significant volumes can be placed without having to worry too much about the possible 'saturation' of investor demand. Second, it has removed opportunities for currency diversification and arbitrage. In search of higher yields, investors now need to focus much more on credit arbitrage than they did in 1998 or earlier years.

A typical example of recent transactions was the LBO of Zeneca Chemicals by Investcorp and Cinven, two private equity companies. They paid a total of DM3.9 bn for a company with DM2.1 bn in sales and profits of DM270 mn. In addition to DM1.5 bn provided in the form of equity, Investcorp and Cinven borrowed DM1 bn as a bridge loan to a junk bond, and received the remainder through senior debt syndicated by Chase Manhattan and J.P. Morgan. The junk bond was launched in July, to yield 500 bp over 10-year US Treasuries.[126]

Margins in this type of deal are attractive indeed, at approximately 200 bp for Zeneca, for example. The average fee earned on junk bond issuance

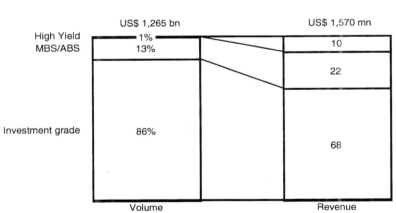

distribution in %, totals US$

Sources: McKinsey, IFR Platinum

Figure 5.2   Issuance and revenues by debt category, 1998

was approximately 180 bp in Europe in 1998. Despite accounting for only 0.7 per cent of total issuance, high-yield bonds probably generated 10 per cent of total revenues (Figure 5.2). Investment banks are therefore adding staff to their LBO teams.[127]

Measures

In the US, high-yield bonds returned an average of 11.5 per cent per year between 1988 and 1998, some 2.4 per cent over the Lehman Brothers corporate bond index. Volatility, however, was high (Figure 5.2). Excess returns on junk bonds were largely driven by the effects of market segmentation.[128] Since many institutions were barred from investing in paper below investment grade, the remainder needed to be overcompensated for the risk they were taking. In many European countries, however, the holding of high-yielding bonds by institutions is not prohibited. At the same time, because of the scarcity of rating on the continent, there is very little experience in buying corporate bonds. Where asset allocation limits are set by law or decree, high-yield is not one of the categories included in the list. Hence, institutional investors are hesitant to buy paper that they are not expressly permitted to hold.

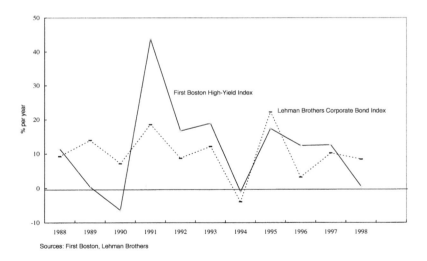

Figure 5.3   Annual return on corporate bonds and high-yield bonds, 1988–98

This suggests that a number of measures could give an important boost to the European high-yield market and help to kick-start corporate restructuring. An improved and expanded rating capacity on the continent, perhaps through a European rating agency, could give an important stimulus to the market for high-yield bonds. Currently, US rating agencies have a near-monopoly in the rating market. In recent years they have focused on recording growth in the Pacific region and Latin America, and Europe has been rather neglected. Also, US-based rating agencies, managed by North American managers, have found it difficult to assess European firms, because they report according to different accounting standards. In the quest for appropriate personnel, rating agencies have found it hard to beat their direct competitors, that is, investment banks and management consultancies. A genuinely European rating agency, providing comprehensive assessments of companies' riskiness and tapping a full range of knowledge about European markets, rules, regulations and cultural idiosyncrasies, could help to develop a more active market for corporate bonds in general. Facilitating the growth of high-yield as well would be a welcome spin-off.

Also, there is a need for research capacity to be set up; it is vital to note here that much of the research that has underpinned the growth of the US's high-yield market is still lacking in Europe. Mike Milken first chanced on the potential of junk bonds at the Wharton School of Finance, when he was working on the returns of 'fallen angels', that is, the corporate bonds of firms that had once been investment-grade. After a major shock, they had lost this stamp of approval. Due to the effects of market segmentation, there appeared to be excess returns, and it was this that convinced him that there might be a market for paper that was 'junk' at the time of issuance. Similar research in Europe has not been carried out, partly because the market for corporate paper is too small. What could usefully be done is the academic analysis of credit default data amassed by the banks over the last decades. Unsurprisingly, they are reluctant to share this information under normal conditions, regarding it as an important source of competitive advantage. There should be some requirement for banks to share aggregate data on default frequencies, and so on, and to report this information to the standard statistical agencies (which can ensure it remains anonymous). Properly collected in anonymous form it could easily be used for academic research, without putting individual banks' competitive positions at risk. European governments should also seriously consider investing in new research institutes in finance. To the present day, this is an almost exclusively US field. Germany's leading research organization, the Max Planck Society, has dedicated research institutes for psycholinguistics (Nijmegen), for iron research (Düsseldorf) and for coal research (Mülheim), but no institute for finance. The benefits would, of course, not be confined to the high-yield market, but further research could be particularly helpful in this area.

Countries with asset class restrictions should, as we argued above, either abolish them, or at least include high-yield bonds in the list of asset classes that can be used. Without such explicit limitation – which is, at the same time, a form of approval for allocations below the maximum – insurance firms and pension funds will remain reluctant to tap the market for corporate high-yield paper.

Further, European governments should impose higher taxes on the higher yields from junk bonds. In most countries, interest income is taxed either at source, or as part of total income. Higher yields on junk bonds would thus incur a higher tax burden, but they do serve a dual purpose. First, they provide a normal return to investors. Second, they compensate for the higher default probability associated with accepting the liabilities of risky borrowers. An investor may receive high returns for some years, only to see the company default when the bond becomes due, giving him a negative return in total. It would therefore be sensible if investors could offset losses from defaults against interest that they received in the past, and if taxes paid on the interest could then be reimbursed. If there are excess returns – even after defaults – in European high-yield bonds, as there are in the US, the taxman will profit anyway; he should not do so because of taxing promised gains that eventually fail to materialize.

The launch of a European high-yield index, modelled on the First Boston High Yield index, could also help to accelerate the market's development. An index would improve transparency in the market, facilitating the decisions of investors and the transparency of pricing new issues. Also, futures written against the index could be used to hedge exposures in high-yield bonds. One might object that this undermines one of the main benefit of junk bond financing, namely the pressure brought on management by creditors. Ultimately, this argument is of limited value. Just as the move from (essentially non-tradable) credits to bonds has improved the clout of outsiders, the ability to hedge and speculate will enhance the incentive effects.

Finally, going private as a form of turning a firm around (before relisting it) should be made easier. This is one of the most common strategies employed by buyout firms and, increasingly, investment banks. Once a minimum number of shares above the absolute majority has been acquired, the remaining minority shareholders can be squeezed out, that is, legally obliged to sell their shares for a reasonable price. This avoids the problem that a significant part of the gains from restructuring will go to shareholders not contributing to it – it solves the freerider problem.[129] In Germany, shareholders who refuse to sell out have to be offered a limited partnership in the new firm.[130] During the turnaround and the asset sales, the company is privately held. Academic studies have examined which firms are most likely to go private. It appears that the companies eventually delisted squandered money on investments that did little to increase shareholder value. Denis found that the stockmarket reacted negatively to 65 per cent of the investment decisions announced by firms that have effectively gone private in the end.[131] Going private also interacts in an important way with the takeover market. It is sometimes argued that delisting is a defensive move by firms that would otherwise become targets. This is possible, but very similar gains accrue to shareholders, who often receive a 40–60 per cent premium over market value as a result of the change in ownership.

Arguably more important than any of these measures that could help to kick-start the process of corporate restructuring and the European high-yield market would be greater harmonization of Europe's wildly different takeover codes and laws. To harness the power of markets for corporate restructuring, these codes and laws should reduce existing barriers to bids, both friendly and hostile, minimize political interference in the process and limit the ability of companies to use 'poison-pills' for their defence. In a piecemeal fashion, some harmonization is already under way. The UK made a major effort to improve practices through the Cadbury Committee; the City Takeover Code is one of the most comprehensive sets of rules governing takeover activity. Recently, following the case of Société Générale de Belgique, Belgium has largely copied the UK code. The Netherlands' securities regulation is quite like the UK model, given the presence of binational firms.[132] Italy has seen a major takeover battle squaring off Telecom Italia and Olivetti. The Draghi law, which came into law in 1998 (named after the treasury director-general, Mario Draghi) provided that a ceiling on owning more than 3 per cent of a privatized firm becomes null and void once an offer for 100 per cent of the shares has been made.[133] In effect, this will allow many other former state companies to become targets for hostile and friendly bids, and the D'Alema government has shown that left-wing parties need not stand in the way of market forces.

In contrast to those countries that have allowed the markets an increasingly free rein, two core European countries stayed aloof. In France the BNP/Paribas/SocGen debacle has highlighted the government's continuing dislike of market-based changes in corporate control. Foreign bidders were also discouraged informally, as the French government preferred domestic consolidation over European integration in financial services. Germany's Krupp/Thyssen deal, in which a hostile bid was effectively undermined by political interference, also demonstrates that convergence towards a refined Anglo-Saxon model cannot be taken for granted.

To remedy these problems presented by a diverse and sometimes market-hostile environment will not be easy. The extent to which different legal traditions still influence shareholders' rights and creditor protection has recently been highlighted in a number of studies.[134] Wholesale reform, such as the passing of a takeover directive or a single European company statute, remain mired in EU politicking. A European FSA, regulating not just the securities markets but also all investment activity from the retail level up, remains a distant ideal. Instead of aspiring to the impossible, real improvements can be made if the Commission focuses on two issues. First, a European takeover directive, making the passing of national legislation mandatory, should be pushed through. Ideally, the competition Commissioner should be involved much more closely than is the case at present; responsibilities could be shared more evenly between the EU's Directorate-General XV (internal market and financial services) and Directorate-General IV (competition). Nationalistic meddling with the takeover directive would then hopefully not be tolerated any more than unapproved subsidies are today. Second, the EU could push for a directive on shareholders' rights. Germany's KonTraG (*Gesetz zur Kontrolle und Transparenz im Unternehmensbereich*), a new law effective from 1999, has shown that even countries with a legal tradition that is radically different from the Anglo-Saxon model can approximate to the 'one share, one vote' ideal. Additional clauses for minority rights, such as the opportunity to sue management in cases of clear negligence, will also be necessary. Harmonization at the EU level would also make it much less cumbersome for investors to examine the different legal conditions in member countries. In the market for corporate control, the rights of shareholders would at least be guaranteed. Rules such as squeeze-out clauses and minority protection in the case of takeover bids, requiring the bidder to tender for 100 per cent of all shares, could be the thin end of the wedge that could transform European corporate governance.

SPIN-OFFS, CARVE-OUTS AND TRACKING STOCKS – A KICK-START FOR CONTINENTAL ECONOMIES?

In most industrialized countries, large corporations account for a steadily declining share of employment and value creation, in spite of a wave of mega-mergers since the mid-1990s. The transition from the days when multinationals seemed to carry all before them, to today, when nimble start-ups can easily attract market capitalizations that far exceed those of long-established rivals, has caused a good deal of pain. However, downsizing, firing people and closing operations, or below-average growth rates, are not the only way in which to manage the process. Firms can often break themselves up, or allow subsidiaries a far greater degree of autonomy. Some of the easier and more efficient ways are, however, barred in many European countries. They are often forced, as a consequence, to search for more indirect – and markedly less efficient – ways of achieving the same aim. Regulatory changes are necessary to remedy the main problems.

Measures and Consequences

There are three ways in which companies can attempt to increase shareholder value by restructuring their assets: spin-offs, carve-outs and tracking stocks. In spin-offs, firms divest their subsidiaries in full, handing the shares in the new firm to its existing shareholders. With carve-outs, the parent company sells some of the subsidiaries' shares and retains a proportion herself. Importantly, the sale of shares is used to attract new shareholders and thus to widen the investor base. For most intents and purposes, the subsidiary becomes an independent company. Tracking stocks, in contrast, are a halfway house: this is a process of tracking the performance of the subsidiary, but no formal change in ownership takes place.

In 1998 in the US, more than 300 companies decided to sell a subsidiary in full. These spin-offs generated significant benefits for all stakeholders. Companies that spin off one of their subsidiaries, such as Ford in the case of Visteon, or AT&T and Lucent and NCR, often see a considerable rise in the market capitalization of the combined entity. AT&T was valued at US$75 bn in 1996, before the split; in January 1998, the combined value exceeded US$150 bn. The benign effect can be observed in many cases. Subsidiaries spun off by their parent companies have increased in value by 26.9 per cent per year, thus outperforming the S&P 500 by almost 10 percentage points (the value for the Russell 2000 was even higher).[135]

In the case of carve-outs, unusually high returns have also been common. In a sample of 119 carve-outs over the years 1985–96, the total return to shareholders was more than double that on the Russell 2000 index in the years 1985–96. While the broadly-based Russell 2000 returned an average of 10.8 per cent over two-year intervals, firms practising carve-outs regularly generated an average return of 51.1 per cent on the subsidiary and 38.2 per cent for the founding firm.

Tracking stocks, however, have done little to improve shareholder value. On average, they have underperformed the S&P 500. Adjusting for the industry composition of the sample changes this conclusion somewhat, but not much. In addition, small sample sizes limit the reliability of the data.

Higher multiples are partly responsible for the rise in share values of spun-off firms, since investors prefer to buy clearly identified, separate risks. Carve-outs have recorded the biggest improvement in p/e multiples: of 25 per cent for the parent company and 30 per cent for the subsidiary (relative to the market). Spin-offs have come second, adding 7 per cent to the parent and 15 per cent to the subsidiary. Tracking stocks have trailed behind. The parent companies have actually lost value, and subsidiaries have increased their multiples by some 20 per cent. What partly underlies this improvement in multiples is increased analyst coverage. Within two years of a spin-off, the number of equity analysts tracking a stock has risen by fully 25 per cent, compared with an average increase over the same period of 2 per cent for other firms. A second factor that has contributed to the increase in p/e multiples has been wider ownership, with the number of institutional investors increasing particularly strongly.[136]

Operating performance has also improved in most subsidiaries. Return on invested capital rose markedly for spin-offs (from 7.4 per cent to 12.9 per cent within two years of the launch) and tracking stocks (from 5.4 per cent to 8.6 per cent); it fell somewhat in the case of carve-outs (from 10.0 per cent to 9.5 per cent). However, total revenue increased by 32 per cent over two years following the carve-out, compared with 7 per cent for firms in the S&P 500.[137]

Crucially, the overall employment effect is also benign. Lucent Technology added 6.8 per cent to total staff numbers over the two years immediately following independence from AT&T. Sabre, after its split from AMR, added 8.7 per cent, and First Data Corporation increased its head-count by 11 per cent.[138]

Higher returns do, however, go hand in hand with higher risks. The averages described above are largely driven by a handful of star performers. The median carve-out actually underperformed the index, returning 8.2 per cent instead of the 12.4 seen in the Russell index. While snapping up carved-out firms can pay handsomely for investors, diversification in this area is even more important than for other investments – while the chances are good that one catches a truly outstanding performer, the risk of ending up with a lemon is also higher than average.

What largely underlies these improvements, then, are not just investors' preferences for clearly defined risk-return profiles. Given the improvements in operating performance, the management of firms and the motivation of staff also appears to improve. There are a number of reasons why the subsidiaries that are either spun off or carved out perform better.

1. *New balance between centre and periphery.* In many cases, fully-owned subsidiaries are captive clients of the mother company, having to pay certain overheads and other forms of remuneration for services provided by the centre, whether they add value or not. Once subsidiaries receive a greater degree of autonomy, they can decide which services they should still source from headquarters, and which should best be bought elsewhere or provided in-house.
2. *Market discipline.* Once the shares have been floated, analysts will cover the firms; its perceived value will be reflected daily in the share price, providing important guidance to management about the potential risks and benefits of its strategy.
3. *Aligning management incentives.* With shares for the former subsidiary publicly traded, share options and other forms of performance-based compensation can be tied to instruments that reflect the performance of operating units more closely, not only – as before – to those of a large and relatively unfocused firm.
4. *Flexibility.* The desire to set up shop often leads to the most talented managers leaving. With carve-outs and spin-offs, they have a chance to assume greater responsibility, without having to climb the corporate ladder at a snail's pace or to face the full risk of starting a new venture.

Taxing Issues and the Road Ahead

If Europe is to benefit from the advantages of firms rejuvenated through spin-offs, carve-outs and tracking stocks, some changes will be necessary. At present, the obstacles to spin-offs, in particular, lead companies to consider tracking stocks. As the preceding section made abundantly clear, these are an inferior option associated with few improvements in operating performance and shareholder value. Indeed, because of tax distortions many continental companies adopt second-best solutions, making it harder for them to maximize shareholder value and improve operating performance

For spin-offs and carve-outs, the main problem concerns hidden reserves. As most continental European accounting systems favour credit protection over investor information, it is almost inevitable that successful companies value their assets below their market prices. This is undesirable for a variety of reasons; in the case of spin-offs, it can cause sudden tax liabilities, making the whole exercise unprofitable. In Germany, when an institution gives its shareholders equity in the new company, the new shares are treated as taxable dividends and not new assets, to be taxed only if there is a capital gain.[139] Solutions are hard to find, as long as the basic tax treatment remains the same. In principle, it should be possible to value the shares of the subsidiary at the book value of the assets transferred, making no change to the book value of the parent company. Then, tax liabilities would only result when the (remaining) shares are sold by the parent company to the public, instead of being distributed to investors. Again, lower rates of corporate taxation – at least on capital gains – would also help, but simpler measures would significantly reduce barriers.[140]

In carve-outs, in particular, where the vast majority of shares remains with the original company, it is a relatively simple rule that is hindering its wider use in Germany. In the US, ownership of at least 80 per cent of all shares allows full tax consolidation of the mother and the new company. In Germany, this is only possible if there is an explicit agreement to return all profits to the founding firm, thus destroying the purpose of carve-outs altogether. Hence, losses in the new firm cannot be set against profits in the founding firm; the overall tax burden increases, and the volatility of results rises. Already, the ministry of finance is considering allowing tax consolidation to be part of the comprehensive overall reform of corporate taxation in 2001.[141] The sooner such a move is made, the faster the benefits of improved corporate governance and organizational flexibility will become apparent.

TAX COMPETITION – LET'S HAVE SOME?

Over the last few years, the term 'tax competition' has often been in the European press. Initially, the new German finance minister, Oskar Lafontaine, vented his anger that not all European countries were happy to impose the same punitive tax rates as Germany, and that, consequently, businesses might relocate operations and staff. That tax is a consideration in decisions on where to invest in new ventures – and, to a lesser extent, where to maintain existing operations – is certainly true. What puzzled many observers was the idea that there might be something inherently unfair or problematic about it. After all, if countries can provide all the important governmental services without the confiscatory fiscal regimes of Germany and other countries, why should this be discouraged? In 1997, the under-secretary at the German finance ministry, Jürgen Stark, criticized the UK for luring investment banking talent with unfair tax advantages. For staff not permanently based (that is, is avoiding becoming permanently resident for tax purposes) in the UK, income tax is only due for those parts of their earnings that are transferred to the UK. Since many high-fliers are also frequent travellers, it used to be quite easy – especially for foreigners and British citizens who had gained expatriate status through extended stays abroad – to avoid establishing a tax residence in the UK. UK income tax can be avoided on those parts of compensation that are saved.[142] The withdrawal of the foreign earnings deduction (FED) in the 1998 UK budget made it in principle considerably harder to escape income tax on foreign earnings. Thus, in terms of tax rules, the playing field is still not level, but has become more so over the last two years. Note, however, that under most double-taxation treaties, personnel with foreign tax residence are liable to pay their taxes in their home countries. The problem does not appear to be that the UK is charging extremely low rates of tax or granting over-generous exemptions, but that it allows the home governments of staff to benefit from the high compensation paid to bankers working in London – if their tax authorities are up to the job.

The unspoken assumption underlying this discussion is that, if competition of this kind goes too far, tax rates may – *horribile dictu* – have to be cut, and some public services may suffer. Ultimately, only immobile assets and incomes can be taxed, whereas highly mobile assets such as capital – along with highly skilled employees – cannot be forced to contribute except marginally to total tax revenue. Overall, of course, average tax takes have not fallen in most OECD countries.

Independent of the flawed logic that is evident in this debate, it is also remarkable for the sense of hopelessness that pervades it. Continental European countries would be unable to compete, it is thought, because they cannot do without the high levels of taxing and spending that they are accustomed to. The argument here is that one of the countries with the most oppressive fiscal regimes could – without major distortions or changes to its tax structure – be highly competitive for the group of specialists which has been at the centre of attention in this book. Partly because of the high rates of income tax, securities houses find it difficult to transfer specialists to continental financial centres. We calculated that London specialists, before they are willing to transfer to Frankfurt, need at least 33 per cent higher salary, and that an important part of this differential is driven by tax considerations as well as more favourable, funded and tax-privileged pension schemes.[143]

Bonuses are an important part of total compensation in investment banking. In 1999, performance-related pay for senior investment bankers (such as heads of equity trading) varied from 24 per cent to 115 per cent of base salary, or £21,000–£185,000, according to a survey by the Monks Partnership. According to some estimates, the annual bonus payout in the City of London can reach up to £800 mn. The highest-paid investment bankers, such as corporate finance heads and fund management directors, also receive the highest proportion of their salaries as bonuses. An important part of this could easily be paid in the form of shares and share options on the employer's stock.

Germany is one of the very few countries where capital gains are not taxed once a security has been held for 12 months. Even the UK and the US, for all their highly developed equity culture, impose much greater fiscal burdens on shareholders. This advantage could be leveraged to attract and retain mobile wealth creators. Following the changes recently introduced as part of a new law (KonTraG), share options can now be granted to management much more easily than before. Although still not common to the extent that they are in the US, German firms are keen to adopt the new compensation instruments. About half of Germany's 100 largest firms are considering the introduction of share option schemes.

A significant proportion of investment banking bonuses could simply be paid in the form of shares and share options, with capital gains accruing to the individual without tax. There would be three main advantages. First, Germany could finally bring down the effective top rate of income tax on the highest earners, which is simply too high at present to attract much talent from abroad. The reduction would be particularly effective if call options are transferred that are initially almost worthless because the underlying asset is priced far below the strike. In part, this would only level

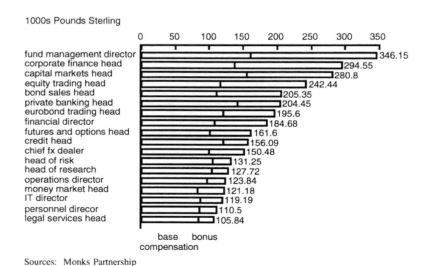

Sources: Monks Partnership

Figure 5.4   Compensation in investment banks, City of London, 1999

the playing field with the UK, where the first £30,000 of executive share options are tax-free (and no limit is applied to options granted before 17 July 1995).[144] In the US also, incentive share options (issued with a strike above the current share price, and held for a minimum of two years) receive favourable tax treatment, being taxed at the rate of capital gains, substantially lower than the top rate of income tax.[145] If good managerial performance, a generally favourable climate in the equity markets, share buy-backs, and so on cause the share price to rise, the capital gain on the option could be completely free of tax once it is held for more than 12 months.[146] For top executives (like senior investment bankers) receiving the average compensation (equivalent to £336,000, or DM1.008 mn), the average tax liability in the UK would be in the range of 38 per cent if no proportion were paid offshore or through options. Under current taxation rules (for a married man, with his wife earning nothing), the average tax to be paid in Germany would equal 51 per cent, that is a 'penalty' of DM126,000 per year. If the bonus component were to be paid in the form of stock options that are out of the money when given, but in the money later, the investment banker in Germany would only have to pay 29.8 per cent of his pre-tax income, saving some DM89,000 relative to his British peer. Nor could this kind of advantage be replicated easily in the UK, where share ownership is much more common, and HM Treasury relies on capital gains tax for a substantial part of revenue. There would be severe shortfalls for the Treasury were the UK to replicate the suggestions for Germany.

In the case of shares being bought on behalf of staff and transferred as part of total compensation, leverage would be much lower. Consequently, the tax efficiency would be markedly less as well. It is especially in those areas where German markets are showing high rates of growth that bonuses and total compensation tend to be high. Frankfurt is largely uncompetitive in forex and futures and options, and should not – as we argued earlier – try to compete. Compensation is only moderate by investment banking standards, however. High rates of income tax do make it harder to attract talent in other areas. It is in corporate finance, capital markets and asset management, where local provision of services can increase their quality as well, that salaries are almost twice as high, and where simple bonus and base compensation payments would be taxed very severely under present conditions. Recent developments in investment banking have made this form of bonus payment technically much more feasible. Over the past 20 years, many of the largest and most respected houses have gone public. From Salomon Brothers to Goldman Sachs, banks have sought to gain an acquisition currency, while at the same time being able to compensate their employees more adequately.

Fiscal revenue would still be generated out of the 47–80 per cent of the salary that is not paid in the form of bonuses. Since this proportion of the salary would have been taxed elsewhere before the transfer of staff, this would augment the domestic fiscal take. At the same time, it is necessary to take into account possible reductions in the tax burden of senior managers already located in Germany before the new measures were passed. The fall in taxes on their income would tend to reduce tax revenue, but nowhere near as strongly as the economically misguided tax benefits for investments in East German property and loss-making container ships. There would also be no distortion to the tax system, which currently already frees all capital gains after a 12-month holding period. The advantage would be that employees' incentives would be much better aligned with those of the firm they are serving. Especially if share ownership is promoted, the relatively long vesting period of 12 months under German capital gains rules will encourage employees to identify and act in the long-term interest of their employer.[147]

Tax competition within Europe, we argue, need not be a bad thing. More importantly, Germany has one important advantage in any competitive race for talent, and that is its highly favourable tax treatment of capital gains. This section suggests that it should leverage this advantage more fully by facilitating the use of shares and share options as part of the total compensation package for senior executives. The reduction in fiscal revenue that would ensue is likely to be small, as losses on the existing tax base will partly be compensated by a higher number of these earners being taxed. The upside is more important: with effective tax rates more in line with that of major competitors, Frankfurt firms could finally avoid part of the large premia for skilled staff that they are having to pay out at present. Higher profits – which, again, would be taxed – would also help to cushion any fall in income tax as a result of this move.

A SINGLE EUROPEAN CAPITAL MARKET

The euro has done much for the development of an integrated European capital market. Debt markets in particular have become deeper and more liquid, supporting a wider range of products. Most spectacularly of all, the market for European corporate bonds has taken off since the launch of the new currency in January 1999. At the same time, full integration remains a long way off. Two major obstacles currently stand in its way: the fragmentation of share and derivatives trading in Europe, and the lack of unified regulatory and supervisory oversight. That exchanges in Europe are a dime a dozen has often been observed. Many an exchange alliance has come to nought, despite all the cost savings and synergies that existed on the drawing board. Market participants are losing their patience. Initiatives for private trading networks have mushroomed in recent months. From Euro MTS to Crossnet, large institutional investors and intermediaries are exploring alternative ways of cutting the cost of multiple trading systems, clearing houses and the limited scope for cross-margining that these imply. The message for traditional stock exchanges is all too clear: shape up or shut down.

Although the fragmentation of trading systems has received ample attention, an equally important obstacle has been highlighted by EMU. Despite the launch of the euro, the further integration of Europe's capital markets is hampered by the multitude of agencies at the national (and sometimes regional) level charged with ensuring fair and orderly markets as well as safeguarding the interests of retail investors. Securities houses operating throughout Europe have to satisfy more than 15 regulators. Cross-listings of shares, despite an EU directive on prospectuses, is still cumbersome and costly. Takeover codes vary from country to country, and the protection of retail investors is organized by an endless array of regulations. The seemingly easiest solution is an EU directive analogous to the one on banking, passed in 1989.[148] Just as banks receive a licence to conduct their business throughout the EU once they have been approved by their national regulator, securities rules and regulations could be invoked universally. This would simply be an extension of the passporting arrangements currently used in the EU, which are, however, restricted to prudential oversight. Two objections can be made. First, this would invite regulatory arbitrage and would lead to inconsistencies in the application of securities law. Second, even seemingly clear and unambiguous documents such as the banking directive have not done much to undermine the unbridled nationalism and interventionist attitude of some national regulators. New directives might help, but experience suggests that a separate authority actually overseeing the implementation of a unified set of capital market regulations will be necessary to ensure conformity and overcome the piecemeal resistance of national bureaucracies.

A number of reasons speak in favour of establishing single national financial services regulators. First, the lines of distinction between different financial services have become increasingly blurred. This is true at the level of firms and of products. From the abolition of the Glass-Steagall Act and the current wave of mergers between brokers and securities houses (epitomized by the Morgan Stanley/Dean Witter deal), to the trend towards bankassurance (CS/Winterthur), the question whether one particular business line is wholesale or retail, insurance or a security transaction, is becoming more and more academic. Why, then, should oversight of financial conglomerates be concentrated in one authority? Just as good risk management should assess the overall risk profile of an institution, regulators should be able to examine the solvency and compliance of firms as a whole. Otherwise, there exists a very real danger that crucial areas are either overlooked entirely, or that muddled responsibilities lead to squabbling between agencies and a lack of clear guidance. In areas of overlap, the establishment of a single authority can help to avoid duplication in compliance efforts. The model practised in many countries with multiple agencies appears to work smoothly. Overall assessments are made by a lead regulator that co-ordinates between different agencies. It would be hard to argue that such an alternative approach has lead to major difficulties. The argument in favour of a single regulator appears to be based on efficiency, not effectiveness. As cross-functional interactions grow in number, the case for concentration at the regulatory level becomes stronger. The UK was not the first country to set up a single financial services regulator.[149] Numerous countries, and in particular Scandinavia, have set up such authorities (Figure 5.5), and Israel, Mexico and South Africa are among the many countries considering such a move.

What are the reasons for extending what appears to be the superior organizational solution at the national level to the international arena? And is Europe the right area to apply it to? The argument in favour at the national level focuses on costs rather than effectiveness. Cross-border conduct of business has grown at least the pace of cross-functional business within countries. Securities firms are arguably amongst the most internationalized companies anywhere. Also, lead regulation appears to work somewhat less well at the international than at the national level: see, for instance, CSFB's recent troubles in Japan or the Barings disaster in Singapore. On the other hand, cultural and legal structures still differ very significantly, even within the EU, making it harder to set up and maintain a single regulator that would be sufficiently close to the markets.[150] On balance, the counter-arguments do not appear to hold much water, while the lack of effective and cost-efficient oversight through the lead regulator model appears to weigh very strongly in favour of a European financial services regulator.

The best model for such an institution is not hard to find. Europe is unique in being able to pick from a very wide range of national experiments. Most professionals in the securities industry have been impressed by London's FSA, which regulates everything from securities markets to investment advice. Despite its sweeping powers, market participants have noted its flexible and informal approach as well as the competence of its staff. Even if some only switched to the FSA after losing their City jobs

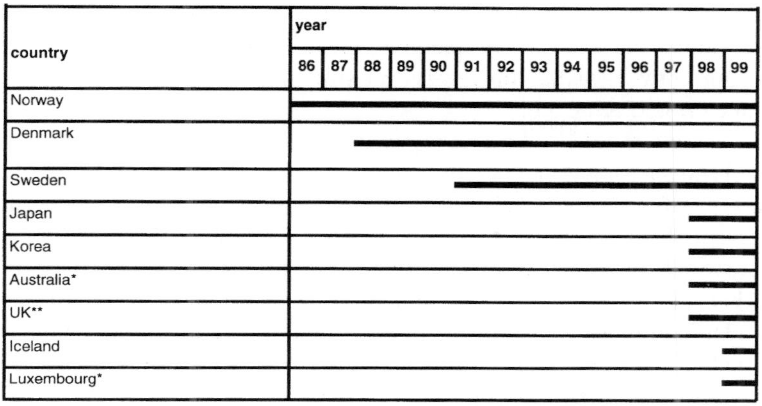

country	year													
	86	87	88	89	90	91	92	93	94	95	96	97	98	99
Norway	██	██	██	██	██	██	██	██	██	██	██	██	██	██
Denmark			██	██	██	██	██	██	██	██	██	██	██	██
Sweden						██	██	██	██	██	██	██	██	██
Japan													██	██
Korea													██	██
Australia*														██
UK**														██
Iceland														██
Luxembourg*														██

* Combines 2 out of 3 main functions (securities industry, retail investment advice and insurance)
** Staff is currently co-located in the same building, but functions have not yet been fully merged. The necessary Act of Parliament is expected to be passed in 2000

Source: FSA

Figure 5.5 Single financial services regulators, by country, 1986–99

(thus suggesting that they may not consistently be the best and brightest in their field), most authorities on the continent do not even pay the salaries that would attract former investment bankers, and often fall woefully short of the kind of professional environment these specialists expect.[151] As a first step, securities markets should be given greater leeway to opt for regulation by just one of the national authorities. National barriers are blurring as exchanges and clearing houses, for example, increasingly co-operate, form alliances or merge. It would be entirely in keeping with the spirit of the EU's banking and ISD directives if European exchanges, operating in more than one country, could opt for being regulated by, say the FSA, and would consequently have a free hand to offer their services throughout the EU area. This would also mark their transition from semi-governmental institutions to profit-oriented companies that they need to become in order to survive into the twenty-first century.

SUMMARY

Much remains to be done to improve the efficiency of European capital markets and centres. Continental countries in particular, saddled with high structural unemployment and slow growth, should actively seek to promote their financial centres. As recent research suggests, larger equity markets and higher valuations may contribute directly to higher productivity growth and a lower 'natural rate' of unemployment.[152] A first impression of the relation between valuation levels and structural unemployment can be gleaned from Figure 5.6.[153]

In many ways the most pressing issue is the highly uneven taxation of mobile talent. Simple and flexible solutions, tailored to the need of financial service staff, can solve most of the difficulties, we argued – a wholesale overhaul of national tax systems is not necessary for our purposes (desirable as it is in its own right). Work on completing the single European capital market through regulatory harmonization is also urgent. It is a bit of a scandal that, more than eight years after the introduction of the common market and after the launch of the euro, there is still no unified, market-friendly framework for Europe's capital markets.

Somewhat less urgent is the issue of 'prudent man' regulation. While the demographic time bomb is slowly undermining Europe's social security systems, unshackling institutional investors is crucial. However, given the magnitudes of possible increases in returns involved, it is far more important to produce well-designed legislation, properly embedded in coherent tax policies, than to rush stop-gap measures into law. The final issue highlighted by us as a policy option concerns the regulatory framework for corporate restructuring. While much more can and needs to

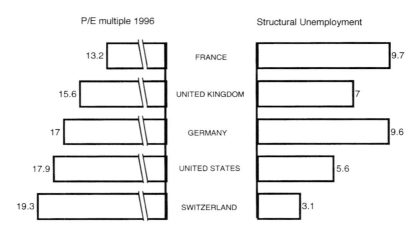

Sources: OECD, Compustat

Figure 5.6   Price/earnings multiples and structural unemployment 1996

be done, the dramatic increase in takeover activity and other restructurings on the continent in 1999 appears to suggest that current conditions are not stifling. Also, relatively small and unproblematic changes – such as Italy's Draghi law – may be sufficient to facilitate the changes already underway.

The five policy areas highlighted in this section will not immediately remedy any of the difficulties faced by financial communities in continental European countries. As we argued in Chapter 4, the persistence of comparative advantage is strong in the case of financial services. Even if all structural problems such as prohibitive tax rates were solved soon, no quantum leap could be expected in a matter of years. The policy initiatives presented in this section need many years to bear fruit. This makes it all the more urgent that their implementation is not delayed unduly.

Notes

1. Crane et al. 1995.
2. Cf. the stimulating analysis in Davis 1990, pp. 18–19. Interestingly, he starts out by asking questions very similar to our own: 'Can the City of London survive as a major financial centre? Or will it absorb much of the business conducted in Paris, Frankfurt, and Amsterdam? Will financial centres soon cease to be necessary, given developments in technology?' A sign that, while some reasons for uncertainty may have changed slightly over the past decade, the level of anxiety certainly has not.
3. Cited in Levine 1997, p. 688.
4. Levine and Zervos 1998, King and Levine 1993, Levine 1997.
5. This is the title of a classic on technological change, Mokyr 1990.
6. Rajan and Zingales 1998.
7. Smith and Walter 1999.
8. Kindleberger 1974, pp. 2, 7.
9. Kindleberger 1974, pp. 6–10; Gershenkron 1962.
10. Only if all countries in question provided detailed and timely statistics on trade in financial services could such an exercise be undertaken. Despite recent advances, the current data is not sufficient for such an exercise.
11. The publications examined were the *FT*, *Institutional Investor*, *Euromoney* and *Options World*. We were unable to obtain figures from Reuters, the other large provider of financial information, since Reuters tends to sell via general contracts, and hence has few terminals that it can trace.
12. The most optimistic indicator for Frankfurt (number of senior staff) gives a ratio that is only 103.7 per cent of the most pessimistic measure. It could be argued that the Bloomberg figures for Frankfurt understate the size of the wholesale sector in Germany. Indeed, while there are no Bloomberg screens in France/the UK outside Paris/London, there are quite a few outside Frankfurt. Including these would raise the total for Germany to 4959 (instead of the 3720 reported for Frankfurt). This would lower London's share to 70.7 per cent, and raise Germany's to 19.7 per cent.
13. Figures for forex trading reported here are 'net-gross', that is, are corrected for local double-counting. Correction for global double-counting is more difficult, and would limit the extent to which current data can be compared with those from earlier periods.
14. Note that some of the change in relative position is simply the result of changes in currency value – the fall in the yen, for example, is partly responsible for lower volumes in Tokyo.
15. ISDA notes that much of the increase in market activity in 1998 was driven by hedging; this may explain why trading activity has failed to expand at the same pace as total market volume. Cf. ISDA 1999.
16. BBA 1998.
17. Credit events refers to the type of occurrence that triggers the contract provisions – in the case of a default swap, for example, it defines what

constitutes an effective default that entitles the buyer of credit protection to compensation.

18. 'Credit Derivatives', *Economist* 13 August 1999.
19. BIS 1999.
20. BBA 1996.
21. BBA 1998, p. 33.
22. Covill 1999.
23. Sherriff 1999.
24. Sherriff 1999.
25. Davidson and Ledger 1998, p. 17; Garrity and O'Leary 1999, p. 22.
26. Liffe 1999. The picture is not changed if we include the 12,620 Eurotop 300 ex-UK contracts traded on LIFFE/AEX.
27. Steil and Pagano 1996.
28. The trading system view only counts transactions that occur within one specific trading system. The regulated environment view is substantially more comprehensive, encompassing all transactions performed by institutions regulated by one authority – even if the transaction took place elsewhere, or on another country's trading system.
29. The Herfindahl index fell from 3655 to 2496. The Gini coefficient can be thought of as the size of the area bounded by the actual curve and the 45 degree line, normalized to complete inequality = 1.
30. Amongst other factors, the author controls for (i) the price of labour (ii) organizational structure, that is, if the stock exchange is part of a joint company with a clearing organization or derivatives exchange, etc. The total model specification is

$$\ln C = \ln\alpha_0 + \alpha_1\ln Y_1 + \alpha_2\ln Y_2 + 0.5\gamma_{11}(\ln Y_1)^2 + 0.5\gamma_{22}(\ln Y_2)^2$$
$$+ \beta_1\ln P_1 + \gamma_{11}(\ln P_1)^2 + \gamma_{12}\ln Y_1 Y_2 + \sum_j\gamma_{ij}\ln P_1\ln Y_j + D$$

where Y_1 is the number of trades, Y_2 is the number of companies listed, P_1 is gross domestic product (GDP) per head, and D is a dummy variable for the case if the cost reported includes those incurred in operating a derivatives exchange or settlement business. Cf. Malkamäki 1999, p. 7.
31. NYSE 1998.
32. Davey 1999.
33. Ideally, we would want to control for changes in value due to market performance, and derive a measure of the percentage of net flows captured by centre. The data currently available does not permit such a subdivision.
34. Note that the numbers given in the Technimetrics Report are significantly higher than the totals emerging from the Euromoney Bank Register. This is because the latter focuses much more clearly on senior staff, whereas Technimetrics tries to provide totals for the whole institutional equity group.
35. Average fee in 1998 was 154 bp, according to the Securities Data Corporation, down almost by 100 bp since 1994. Cf. also Garrity and O'Leary 1999.
36. Taking the full fees into account, not just the retained margins.
37. Merchant 1999.
38. Depfa Research 1999, p. 11.

39. Depfa Research 1999, p. 9.
40. Note, however, that the change in relative position is largely driven by a rise in equity valuations; it is not clear that these will continue in the future.
41. There is some evidence to suggest that the US share is procyclical, that is, that is rises whenever the global market as a whole expands rapidly.
42. Of course, in part, higher fee levels simply offset higher costs. Since M&A requires little other than people, higher income taxes are partly to blame in continental Europe.
43. Smith and Walter 1999.
44. Fairlamb 1999.
45. Walker 1999a, 1999b.
46. Covill 1999.
47. In the 4th edition of the IMF-BMP manual, labour and non-financial property income was grouped together with service earnings other than shipment. The 5th edition makes a clear distinction between transactions in income and in services. Cf. OECD 1998b.
48. Financial services and insurance include financial intermediary and auxiliary services conducted between residents and non-residents. Included are intermediary service fees, such as those associated with letters of credit, bankers' acceptances, line of credit, financial leasing and foreign exchange. For the latter, the difference between the midpoint rate and the buying/selling rate is the service charge. Also included are commissions and other fees related to transactions in securities: brokerage, placements of issues, underwriting, redemptions and arrangements of swaps, options and other hedging instruments; commissions of commodity futures traders; and services related to asset management, financial market operational and regulatory services, security custody services, etc. Service charges on purchases of IMF resources are included amongst an economy's financial service payments, as are charges associted with undrawn balances under standby or extended arrangements with the IMF. Financial intermediation services indirectly measured are excluded. Cf. OECD 1998b, p. 9.
49. It should be added that many of the financial services exports from the UK appear to be conducted via the subsidiaries of houses located elsewhere. It could be argued that, for example, continental banks have a powerful incentive to use distorted transfer prices, hence generating higher cost in high-tax locations (such as Germany), and producing profits where taxes are lower, that is, the UK. Note, however, that the US is an even larger customer for London's financial services, despite actually offering at least equally competitive tax rates.
50. Note, however, that the Swiss figures do not appear to square fully with the UK export figures, which show Switzerland as a major customer.
51. Includes trade in insurance products.
52. Note that figures for trade in financial services also include insurance. Only for the UK is it easily possible to distinguish between the two types of service.
53. Germany's share in manufacturing exports is 9.7 per cent, which would be equivalent to US$6.7 bn in exports. This would – given constant imports – yield a surplus of US$3.6 bn. Average value added in financial services in

the US in 1997 was US$203,000 per employee. If German productivity were lower, the corresponding figure for employment would be higher.

54. Some of the earliest and most interesting observations on trade in financial services can be found in Arndt 1984, 1988.
55. Krugman 1990.
56. Franks et al. 1998, p. 1558.
57. Schwab and Sachs 1999.
58. Note that financial service exports are not on the same systematic level as the other product areas enumerated – they represent a summary measure of competitiveness in all traded financial services.
59. Note that we do not use identical reference periods due to data constraints. To compensate, the rates of change are annualized. As the purpose is to compare centres, the resulting bias is probably irrelevant.
60. Firms in the second category are Bear Sterns, JP Morgan, Morgan Stanley; the unadjusted sample contains Alex Brown, Bear Sterns, JP Morgan, Lehman Brothers, Morgan Stanley, Salomon Smith Barney, Salomon Brothers and Bankers Trust.
61. World Bank 1999, table 5.4, p. 284.
62. Counting trading volumes is notoriously difficult because of two problems: double counting of trades (as in the case of forex and other transactions), and two main approaches to counting transactions (the trading system view as opposed to the regulated environment view). We rely here on the statistics compiled by the IMF/IFC, which take these two factors into account.
63. Jorion and Goetzmann 1999.
64. Note, however, that the UK and the US include consumer durables in measures of household wealth.
65. Of course, higher rates of income growth since the second world war are partly responsible for the difference as well; saving out of past (lower incomes) will appear smaller relative to incomes today. It would hence be heroic to indict continental financial systems on the basis of this measure alone.
66. Calculated as the change in household wealth net of the savings inflow. We therefore abstract from the effect of asset sales; the calculated rates are a lower bound on the true rate of return. As long as the ratio of asset sales to household wealth is relatively constant across countries, this should not bias our results. In recent years, there has been some indirect evidence that there is a wealth effect in the US, and, to a lesser extent, in the UK. On the continent, it is much smaller, and has certainly not been reflected in consumer spending. If this potential source of error is relevant, it will impart a downward bias to the figures for the UK and the US.
67. Note that, due to the effects of reunification and other changes in the compilation of this statistic, use of the longer series is problematic.
68. Variation in the German data is less meaningful since the run of years is relatively short.
69. The combination of relatively high leverage and slow asset growth is probably best explained by the unusually high share of 'real' wealth in portfolios – arguably a result of distortions in the housing market.
70. Note that the German figures may also have suffered from the massive flight to tax havens after the introduction of withholding taxes in the late 1980s.

71. Some might argue that it is counter-intuitive to count a high savings rate as a 'liability', not a plus. Note, however, that for any given increase in assets, people will be better off if they managed to achieve it without having to save more.

72. The French figures appear too high from our point of view; the OECD statistics division is unable to clarify the matter and failed to respond to numerous enquiries.

73. Total equity holdings, including foreign holdings.

74. According to calculations of the DAI (1999), at the end of 1998, Germans held 8.7 per cent of their total liquid assets in equities. The definition of the base used here is different from the OECD one. Between 1997 and 1998, the proportion increased by 0.4 per cent.

75. Defined as the ratio of financial assets to net financial wealth.

76. Obstfeld and Taylor 1998, p. 358.

77. The countries are UK, Germany, France, Austria, Belgium, Netherlands, Ireland, Italy and Denmark.

78. Hardouvelis, Malliaropoulos and Priestley (1999, pp. 30–2) calculate that local risk decreased, lowering financing costs by 3.1 per cent, while the importance of total market risk increased, driving cost up by one per cent.

79. Berglöf 1997.

80. Edwards and Fischer 1994.

81. Kaplan 1994a, 1994b.

82. The χ^2-statistics for income is significant at the 98 per cent level, while in the case of sales, the difference between observed and expected values is not significant at any customary rejection level.

83. The χ^2-statistic is significant at the 95 per cent level.

84. It could be argued that deviations of performance measures from their long-term mean should be better predictors. If such a calculation is carried out, the proportion of UK CEOs losing their job compared with the expected value is large, at 30 per cent higher than expected.

85. Either through lower consumption (because of higher investment and depreciation), or because of reductions in leisure.

86. Note, however, that a recent OECD paper (Nicoletti 1998) using cyclically adjusted figures suggests that France continues to lag US labour productivity by 5 per cent, Germany by 14 per cent, Switzerland by 17 per cent and the UK by 37 per cent.

87. McKinsey Global Institute 1996, 1997.

88. McKinsey Global Institute 1996, 1997.

89. This is true for trends over time in any one country. Between-country variation is also strongly influenced by the extent to which legal and other factors permit operating flexible shiftwork arrangements.

90. Note that we are not controlling for the state of the business cycle; since Germany was still enjoying the post-unification boom in the early 1990s, whereas the US was experiencing a sharp recession, some of the increase in the gap may be attributable to the more favourable state of the cycle in the US.

91. Note also that most of the growth comes from higher productivity, not greater factor intensity.

92. Francois and Schuknecht 1999.

93. The phrase '*Le Prix de L'Euro*' is taken from a recent paper by Lascelles (1999b).
94. Note that attaining benchmark status is also sometimes thought to be a result of having large, liquid, open asset markets in a country. Cf. Frenkel and Goldstein 1999.
95. Lascelles 1999a, 1999b.
96. Johnson et al. 1999.
97. The celebrated case of the QWERTY keyboard is controversial (David 1997; Liebowitz and Margolis 1990). At the same time, there are few who seriously would argue that QWERTY-style processes are unimportant in cases such as the adoption of VHS over Betamax, or the victory of Windows over Macintosh OS.
98. OECD 1998a, annex table 63, p. 253. Sceptics may argue that our argument about the benign effects of efficient capital markets is undermined by this evidence. Note, however, that manufacturing is only a small part of the economy in most countries now. Even in Germany, the service sector as a whole is larger. Manufacturing does, however, have a disproportionate share of exports and imports. Although service-sector performance has great weight for overall economic efficiency, it is still largely manufactured goods that account for most exports.
99. In this sense, they are remarkably similar to currencies' role as international reserve currencies – a preoccupation for politicians, but hardly of any benefit to the economies in question. Cf. Krugman 1999.
100. The gains may be modest, given the present tendency to concentrate equity analysts in one centre.
101. Cited in O'Brien 1992.
102. Cited in Lascelles 1999a.
103. Lascelles 1999a.
104. BoE 1999.
105. Fairlamb 1999, p. 37.
106. Lascelles 1999a, p. 15.
107. Luce 1999.
108. Wilde 1999.
109. Goldman Sachs 1998.
110. Cited in Fairlamb 1999.
111. Lascelles 1999a, p. 12.
112. Fairlamb 1999.
113. Mattern et al. 1997.
114. Kynaston 1997.
115. Note that the powers of the FSA will substantially exceed even those granted to the SEC. Cf. 'Beware of the Watchdog', *Economist* 26 June 1999.
116. The countries classified as 'prudent man' are the Netherlands, the US, the UK, Australia, Canada and Ireland; Belgium, Denmark, France, Germany, Italy, Japan, Portugal, Spain, Sweden and Switzerland have asset restrictions.
117. Burroughs and Helyar 1991.
118. Morck et al. 1988, 1989.
119. Denis and Denis 1995.
120. Mikkelson and Partch 1997.

121. Mikkelson and Partch 1997.
122. Nuttall 1999; Bond et al. 1998.
123. Achleitner and Müller-Trimbusch 1999.
124. 'Moneyed Men in Institutions', *Economist* 6 November 1999.
125. Achleitner and Müller-Trimbusch 1999.
126. Ostrovsky 1999.
127. Ostrovsky 1999.
128. This is just one of the many explanations offered. Cf. Müller-Trimbusch 1999.
129. Achleitner 1999, pp. 555, 566.
130. Covill 1999.
131. Denis 1992.
132. Berglöf 1997, p. 108.
133. Law 474, governing the privatization of formerly state-owned firms, gave the treasury the power to veto any acquisition of shares that would allow individual shareholders to control more than 3 per cent of all equity. Cf. Walker 1999b.
134. La Porta et al. 1998, 1999.
135. Anslinger et al. 1999.
136. Anslinger et al. 1999.
137. Anslinger et al. 1997.
138. The figures are from Datastream.
139. During the minimum 12-month holding period.
140. Cf. Seifert and Voth 1999.
141. Ministry of Finance (Müller-Gartermann), private communication, 28 July 1999.
142. Knipp 1997.
143. In the UK, employees can contribute 17.5–40 per cent of their compensation tax-free to their pension scheme, depending on age.
144. Options granted before 1995 are taxed on the basis of capital gain, that is, using the same tax rate as income tax, but with the option to use the capital gains exemption. Since 1995, they are taxed as income after they are exercised.
145. Schnabel 1998.
146. For incentive reasons, it is often thought better to specify outperformance relative to the market or a sector index.
147. Share options are often thought to encourage excessive risk-taking, since the downside is strictly limited, whereas the upside is not.
148. 'No SECs Please, We're European', *Economist* 21 August 1999.
149. The Act of Parliament will probably only be passed in 2000. Cf. Briault 1999.
150. Briault 1999, p. 16.
151. 'No SECs Please, We're European', *Economist* 21 August 1999.
152. Phelps 1999; Levine and Zervos 1998.
153. Of course, a comprehensive examination of the issue would require a fully specified multifactorial model, giving full credit to factors such as labour market reform.

References

Achleitner, A.-K., ed., *Handbuch Investment Banking* (Wiesbaden 1999).

Achleitner, A.-K. and J. Müller-Trimbusch, 'Der deutsche Markt für High-Yield Unternehmensanleihen', *Finanzbetrieb* 5 (1999).

Anslinger, P., D. Carey, K. Fink and C. Gagnon, 'Equity Carve-outs: A New Spin on the Corporate Structure', *McKinsey Quarterly* (1997).

Anslinger, P., S. Klepper and S. Subromaniam, 'Breaking Up is Good to Do', *McKinsey Quarterly* (1999).

Arndt, H., 'Measuring Trade in Financial Services', *Banca Nazionale del Lavoro Quarterly Review* 149 (1984).

Arndt, H., 'Comparative Advantage in Trade in Financial Services', *Banca Nazionale del Lavoro Quarterly Review* 151 (1988).

Bank of England (BoE), *Practical Issues Arising from the Euro,* June (London 1999).

Berglöf, E., 'Reforming Corporate Governance: Redirecting the European Agenda', *Economic Policy: A European Forum* 24 (1997).

BIS, *Central Bank Survey of Foreign Exchange and Derivatives Market Activity* (Basle 1998a).

BIS, *Quarterly Review – International Banking and Financial Market Developments* (Basle 1998b).

BIS, *69ᵗʰ Annual Report* (Basle 1999).

Bond, S., C. Meghir and F. Windmeijer, 'Productivity, Investment and the Threat of Takeover', unpublished manuscript, Institute for Fiscal Studies (London 1998).

Briault, C., 'The Rationale for a Single National Services Regulator', *FSA Occasional Paper* Series 2 (1999).

British Bankers' Association (BBA), *Credit Derivatives Report 1996. Based on a Survey of the London Market* (London 1996).

British Bankers' Association, *Credit Derivatives Report 1997/98. Based on a Survey of the London and Global Markets* (London 1998).

Burroughs, B. and J. Helyar, *Barbarians at the Gate* (1999)

Covill, L., 'Nascent Opportunities. Overseas Investors have Flooded into a Market Which the German Banks Traditionally had to Themselves', *Financial Times* 11 June (1999).

Crane, D. et al., *The Global Financial System. A Functional Perspective* (Cambridge, MA 1995).

DAI, 'Aktien auf dem Vormarsch', press report (Frankfurt, 9 July 1999).

Davey, E., 'Shifting Values', *Futures and OTC World* 8 (1999).

David, P.A., 'Path Dependence and the Quest for Historical Economics', Oxford University Working Paper in Economic History 20 (1997).

Davidson, J. and A. Ledger, 'European Wholesale Banking post EMU: Feast or Famine?', McKinsey Internal Research Document (London 1998).

Davis, E.P., 'International Financial Centres – An Industrial Analysis', *Bank of England Discussion Paper* 51 (1990).

DBAG, *Fact Book* (Frankfurt various years).

Denis, D., 'Corporate Investment Decisions and Corporate Control: Evidence from Going Private Transactions', *Financial Management* 21 (1992).

Denis, J. and D. Denis, 'Performance Changes Following Top Management Dismissals', *Journal of Finance* 50 (1995).

Depfa Research, *Rentenmarkt*, Research Report 2 (1999).

Economist, 'Beware of the Watchdog', 16 June (1999).

Economist, 'Credit Derivatives', 13 August (1999).

Economist, 'No SECs Please, We're European', 21 August (1999).

Economist, 'Moneyed Men in Institutions', Schools Brief, 6 November (1999).

Edwards, J. and K. Fischer, *Banks, Finance and Investment in Germany* (Cambridge 1994).

Fairlamb, D., 'Dueling Markets', *Institutional Investor* 5 (1999).

Francois, J. and L. Schuknecht, 'Trade in Financial Services: Procompetitive Effects and Growth Performance', *CEPR Discussion Paper* No. 2144 (1999).

Franks, J., S. Schaefer, and M. Staunton, 'The Direct and Compliance Costs of Financial Regulation', *Journal of Banking and Finance* 21 (1998).

Frenkel, J. and M. Goldstein, 'The International Role of the Deutsche Mark', in Deutsche Bundesbank, ed., *Fifty Years of the Deutsche Mark. Central Bank and the Currency in Germany since 1948* (Oxford 1999).

Garrity, B. and C. O'Leary, 'Relentless Forces Erode Fee Structure', *Investment Dealers' Digest* (1999).

Gershenkron, A., *Economic Backwardness in Historical Perspective* (Cambridge, MA 1962).

Goldman Sachs, *The Goldman Sachs/Watson Wyatt EMU Survey* (London 1998).

Hardouvelis, G., D. Malliaropoulos and R. Priestley, 'EMU and European Stock Market Integration', *CEPR Discussion Paper* No. 2124 (1999).

Heidrick and Struggles, *Is Your Board Fit for the Global Challenge? Corporate Governance in Europe 1999 Survey* (Brussels 1999).

ISDA, *Flash Survey 1998* (http://www.isda.org./d1.html) (1999).

Johnson, B. et al., *1999 Index of Economic Freedom* (Washington, DC 1999).

Jorion, P. and W. Goetzmann, 'Global Stock Markets in the Twentieth Century', *Journal of Finance* 54 (1999).

Kaplan, S., 'Top Executive Rewards and Firm Performance: A Comparison of Japan and the US', *Journal of Political Economy* (1994a).

Kaplan, S., 'Top Executives, Turnover and Firm Performance in Germany', *Journal of Law, Economics and Organization* (1994b).

Kindleberger, C. P., 'The Formation of Financial Centres: A Study in Comparative Economic History', *Princeton Studies in International Finance* (Princeton 1974).

King, R. and R. Levine, 'Finance and Growth: Schumpeter Might be Right', *Quarterly Journal of Economics* 108 (1993).

Knipp, T., 'Investmentbanker werden umworben. London lockt Ausländer mit lockeren Steuerregeln', *Handelsblatt* 104 (1997).

Krugman, P., *Rethinking International Trade* (Cambridge, MA 1990).

Krugman, P., 'Who's Afraid of the Euro?', *Fortune Magazine* 27 April (1999).

Kynaston, D., *LIFFE – A Market and Its Makers* (London 1997).

La Porta, R. et al., 'Law and Finance', *Journal of Political Economy* (1998).

La Porta, R., F. Lopez-de-Silanes and A. Shleifer, 'Corporate Ownership Around the World', *Journal of Finance* 54 (1999).

Lascelles, D., 'Confidence in the City Outside the Euro', *New Europe* (London 1999a).

Lascelles, D., 'Le Prix de L'Euro', Centre for the Study of Financial Innovation (London 1999b).

Levine, R., 'Financial Development and Economic Growth: Views and Agenda', *Journal of Economic Literature* 35 (1997).

Levine, R. and S. Zervos, 'Stock Markets, Banks and Economic Growth', *American Economic Review* 88 (1998).

Liebowitz, S. and S. Margolis, 'The Fable of the Keys', *Journal of Law and Economics* (1990).

LIFFE, 'Liffe trades £263 bn per day in June 1999', press release, 2 July (1999).

Luce, E., 'Bonded to a Bright Future', *Financial Times* 14 June (1999).

McKinsey Global Institute (MGI), *Capital Productivity* (Washington, DC 1996).

McKinsey Global Institute, *Removing Barriers to Growth and Employment in France and Germany* (Washington, DC 1997).

Malkamäki, M., 'Are There Economies of Scale in Stock Exchange Activities?', *Bank of Finland Discussion Papers* 4 (1999).

Mattern, F., W. G. Seifert, C. C. Streit, and H.-J. Voth, *Aktie, Arbeit, Aufschwung. Wie der Finanzplatz Wirtschaft und Gesellschaft wieder in Schwung bringen kann* (Frankfurt 1997).

Merchant, K., 'A Triumph of Hope over Experience', *Financial Times* 11 June (1999).

Mikkelson, W. und M. Partch, 'The Decline of Takeovers and Disciplinary Managerial Turnover', *Journal of Financial Economics* 44 (1997).

Mokyr, J., *The Lever of Riches: Technological Creativity and Economic Progress* (Oxford 1990).

Monks Partnership, *International Banks and Investment Houses. Remuneration Guide* (London 1999).

Mork, R., A. Shleifer and R. Vishny, 'Characteristics of Targets of Hostile and Friendly Takeovers', in J. Auerbach, ed., *Corporate Takeovers: Causes and Consequences* (Chicago 1988).

Mork, R., A. Shleifer and R. Vishny, 'Alternative Mechanisms for Corporate Control', *American Economic Review* 79 (1989).

Müller-Trimbusch, J., 'High Yield Anleihen als besondere Form der Risikofinanzierung. Eine Analyse innovativer Fremdfinanzierung deutscher Wachstumsunternehmen am Kapitalmarkt'. PhD thesis, European Business School (Oestrich-Winkel 1999).

Nicoletti, G., 'Performance and Regulation Patterns in OECD countries', OECD, manuscript (Paris 1998).

Nuttall, R., 'An Empirical Analysis of the Effects of the Threat of Takeover on UK Company Performance', *Nuffield Economics Working Paper* W5 (1999).

NYSE, *Factbook 1998* (New York 1998).

O'Brien, R., *Global Financial Integration: The End of Geography* (London 1992).

Obstfeld, M. and A. Taylor, 'The Great Depression as a Watershed: International Capital Mobility in the Long Run', in M. Bordo, C. Goldin, E. White, eds, *The Defining Moment. The Great Depression and the American Economy in the Twentieth Century* (Chicago 1998).

OECD, *Economic Outlook* (Paris various years).

OECD, *Institutional Investors in the New Financial Landscape* (Paris 1998a).

OECD, *Services Statistics on International Transactions 1987–96* (Paris 1998b).

Ostrovsky, 'LBOs Lever Cash to High-Yield Bonds', *Financial Times* 16 July (1999).

Phelps, E., 'Behind This Structural Boom', *American Economic Review, Papers and Proceedings* 89 (1999).

Rajan, R. and L. Zingales, 'Financial Dependence and Growth', *American Economic Review* 88 (1998).

Schnabel, H., 'Wertorientierte Vergütung von Führungskräften'. PhD thesis, University of Cologne (Wiesbaden 1998).

Seifert, W.G. and H.-J. Voth, 'Disziplin statt Konsens: Übernahmen und die Nachteile des deutschen Corporate Governance Modells', in W.G. Seifert and R. von Rosen, *Die Übernahme börsennotierter Unternehmen* (Frankfurt 1999).

Sherriff, D., 'Let a Thousand Yield Curves Bloom', *Euromoney* March (1999).

Smith, R. and I. Walter, '1998 Global Capital Market Activity and Market Shares of Leading Competitors', *New York University Salomon Center Working Paper* S-99–11 (1999).

Steil, B. and M. Pagano, 'Equity Trading I: The Evolution of European Trading Systems', in B. Steil, ed., *The European Equity Markets. The State of the Union and an Agenda for the Millennium* (London 1996).

Walker, M., 'Europe Plays the Takeover Game', *Euromoney* 5 (1999a).

Walker, M., 'The Sack of Telecom Italia', *Euromoney* 7 (1999b)

Wilde, H., 'EMU shuffles the rankings', *Euromoney* 5 (1999).

World Bank, *Development Indicators* (Oxford various years).

Index

reunification, 71
risk, xv, 1, 20, 21, 60, 65, 66, 70, 74,
    81, 94, 106, 108, 110, 111, 113,
    116, 117, 122, 130

Salomon Smith Barney, 49, 101, 127
savings rate, 69, 72, 73
settlement, 24, 28, 34, 99, 100, 102
spin-off, 117, 120, 121
stock options, 127
swaps, 13, 17, 18, 20, 23, 134 n17

talent, xv, 4, 5, 8, 9, 91, 95, 96, 97,
    117, 124, 126, 128, 132
Target, 99, 100, 101
Taurus, 90
taxation
    capital gains, 126

corporate, 124
income, xv, xvi, 90, 124, 125, 126,
    128
Tecnost, 114
Telecom Italia, 16, 99, 114, 119
Thyssen/Krupp, 119
Travellers Salomon Smith Barney, 49,
    101, 105, 107, 127

unemployment, 131

value added, 2, 6, 8, 9, 23, 50, 53, 59,
    60, 61, 88, 95, 96, 104, 106
volatility, 67, 68, 73, 74, 124

World Bank, 1, 2, 3, 29, 39, 53, 86

Xetra, 29, 34